EXPLORING CAREERS IN MUSIC

Compiled by

PAUL BJORNEBERG
Director, American Music Conference

American Music Conference

Music Educators National Conference

The Music Educators National Conference and
the American Music Conference are grateful to
all the organizations and individuals who assisted
in compiling this book.

This book is a revised and expanded version of *Careers in Music*,
published in 1976 by the American Music Conference.

CONTENTS

INTRODUCTION

Is a career in music for you? In this book, we will try to help you decide by examining the wide variety of job possibilities in teaching music in schools and independently, performing popular music, retailing, manufacturing, distributing, publishing, and piano tuning. You will read about band, orchestra, and choral directing; performing with symphony orchestras and armed forces music groups; composing and arranging; arts administration; working in the recording industry; music for worship; music therapy; writing music criticism; communications jobs involving music; and working in music libraries.

To the many thousands of people working in the music business, a career in music is not just a job; it is a fun, exciting, fulfilling, and satisfying way to earn a living.

Of course, there are frustrations and disappointments as in any business field, and we will be as candid as possible, telling you about the pitfalls and potential for success in each career area. We hope you will be as honest with yourself in realistically assessing your own qualities and talents.

While we will be reviewing a number of career possibilities, we will not be able to include the almost endless variations in each.

At the end of each chapter, you will find sources for additional information. Addresses and phone numbers for these and other sources are listed in the directory at the end of the book. You may want to check with these individuals or organizations, as well as talk with your school guidance counselor, the dean of music at a local or state university or college, or anyone you know in the career area you would like to enter. Your school or public library may also have many of the trade publications relating to different aspects of the music field.

Even if you eventually decide on a job outside the music industry, remember that music study and participation are their own rewards. Learning or knowing how to sing or to play a musical instrument helps

1

develop skills and understanding that will pay you handsome dividends, regardless of the career you finally select, and provides a great source of enjoyment throughout life, which is why this country has nearly 57 million amateur musicians.

The advice in this book is not meant to overly encourage or discourage you, only to give you enough information so that you will know what to expect. If you have the talent, determination, and perseverance to work toward your goal, you can succeed. There is room in the music industry for everyone who really wants to make it.

CAREERS IN
PERFORMING ARTS

Symphony Orchestras

Symphony orchestras are a multimillion-dollar industry and offer many opportunities for professional careers.

With expanding services and budgets, orchestras need well-trained artistic and administrative personnel. Although performance positions with many American orchestras are still extremely competitive, more opportunities are available now than ever before. Musicians today can earn a substantial livelihood as orchestral players. Openings for conductors also have increased with the growth in the number of orchestras. Talented administrators have expanded audiences, creating more demand for festivals, concerts, new music, and original instrumental performance groups.

PERFORMING

American orchestras provide a wide range of job opportunities, from part-time work with largely volunteer community orchestras to full-time employment with professional orchestras.

Major orchestras offer musicians and principal players full-time employment with weekly minimum salaries. Most metropolitan orchestras have seasons of forty or fifty-two weeks, which may include youth concerts, tours, and summer or pops engagements, in addition to the regular subscription series.

Orchestras with small budgets generally employ musicians on a weekly basis, a per-service basis, or a combination of both. Organizations in this category differ widely in the number and type of concerts they perform. They often perform chamber and ensemble concerts in addition to full-orchestra concerts. As few as ten or as many as one hundred performances a year may be given by the full orchestra.

Some of these orchestras employ a core ensemble or quartet on a full-time basis, which is augmented by musicians hired on a per-service basis to accommodate the larger symphonic repertoire. Others may retain a full-size orchestra on a limited-season contract and divide personnel for various services. Professional chamber orchestras usually fall into this category, but these generally have longer seasons and pay higher salaries than full symphony orchestras.

Most urban and community orchestras with budgets under $250,000 hire musicians on a per-service basis, and annual salaries depend on the number of concerts given. Most musicians in these orchestras hold other full-time jobs or supplement their salaries with independent teaching.

Sometimes these part-time orchestra positions are offered in conjunction with college or school faculty positions. Musicians working in a large metropolitan area can derive a major part of their income from playing with several community and chamber orchestras, each having a limited number of performances. Community orchestras may pay musicians on a per-service basis or may only pay section leaders and concertmasters, with the majority of musicians being volunteers.

Recommended Preparation

Professional symphony musicians need years of private instrumental study before beginning conservatory-level training. While completion of a degree program is not essential, most orchestral musicians today have conservatory or university training.

It is wise to get as much ensemble experience as possible before entering college; youth orchestras and summer music camps offer excellent opportunities. Apprenticeships with smaller, semiprofessional orchestras also will help expand your orchestral repertoire before you audition for a professional position.

The Tanglewood Music Center's summer Fellowship Program in Lenox, Massachusetts, offers young instrumentalists intensive instruction in orchestral and chamber music and an opportunity to work with well-known musicians. All students chosen to participate in the program receive fellowships to cover full tuition costs.

Interlochen Arts Academy's National Music Camp provides training on all orchestral and band instruments for students ages eight through high school during its eight-week summer program, which offers many performance opportunities and an extensive study of music literature. Interlochen, a college preparatory school for grades 9–12 offers training in all forms of music with performance opportunities on the Interlochen campus and on tour.

The Aspen Music School offers an opportunity to play with a variety of orchestral ensembles during a four-, five-, or nine-week session each summer. The Festival Orchestra and the Chamber Symphony consist of young professionals and students whose services are contracted through auditions.

The Aspen Sinfonia, Concert Orchestra, and Philharmonia are all formed from the student body. Students may attend classes in music literature and theory and take private instrumental lessons and master classes from noted performers. More than 80 percent of the students receive some financial assistance. A new program, the first of its kind, founded in 1988 by Ruben Gonzalez, co-concertmaster of the Chicago Symphony, is the Orchestral Leadership Seminar. This seminar is designed to provide specialized training for current and prospective concertmasters.

Many American universities and conservatories are well known for training orchestral musicians, among them the Eastman School of Music, the Manhattan School of Music, the Conservatory of Music at Oberlin College, The Juilliard School, The Curtis Institute, New England Conservatory, Indiana University, Yale University, the Cleveland Institute, and the College-Conservatory of Music at the University of Cincinnati. Training opportunities are available at orchestras such as the New World Symphony in Miami, Florida, and YMF Debut Orchestra in Los Angeles. Extracurricular opportunities also are available through summer music camps provided by groups such as the Interlochen Festival of Music in Michigan and the Music Festival of Florida in Sarasota.

The Shepherd School of Music, at Rice University in Houston, offers a curriculum to train musicians for symphony orchestra careers. The focus of the five-year Orchestral Studies Program (which combines bachelor's- and master's-degree study) is the school's orchestra, which meets regularly both as a full orchestra and in small coaching groups. Students also receive background in music theory, history, and applied studies.

CONDUCTING

Although competition for conducting positions with major orchestras is fierce, there is a continuing opportunity with smaller orchestras, particularly community orchestras. In addition, the expansion of services provided by major orchestras has opened up a new field of secondary positions.

The chief conductor of an orchestra may direct from 30 percent to 80 percent of the subscription concerts and make a number of guest conducting appearances in other cities. If a conductor is the music director, he or she generally has full responsibility for artistic decisions in addition to conducting duties.

Conducting staffs of large professional orchestras also may include any of the following: resident conductor, principal guest conductor, and associate and assistant conductors whose primary responsibilities are often pops or youth concerts. Some staffs include a conducting assistant who occasionally conducts.

Conductors of many small professional orchestras include those who conduct community, college, and youth orchestras. They generally hold these posts in conjunction with other full- or part-time positions as college or school music teachers, as musicians with larger symphonies, or as independent music instructors. In many community symphonies, the music director also assumes managerial duties when the orchestra does not have a professional manager.

Recommended Preparation

Since the conductor must be a well-developed musician, substantial experience as a performer, particularly with ensembles and orchestras, is essential. (Youth, high school, and college orchestras offer early playing experiences.) College or conservatory music study, including choral and instrumental conducting and orchestration courses, as well as a solid background in music history and performance practices, is also a requirement. In college, an aspiring conductor should get as much experience as possible directing student ensembles. Score-reading ability and a well-developed ear are important. Keyboard facility, particularly orchestral reduction, is useful.

Aspiring conductors should continually expand their exposure to live and recorded performances of all types of music. They should know not only the symphonic repertoire but all forms of musical expression. Personality is important; vitality and leadership ability should be coupled with fine musicianship.

Getting Experience

A great deal of conducting experience can be gained by working with college or conservatory student ensembles, with small community orchestras on a volunteer basis, or with youth orchestras at one of more than three hundred summer music camps in the United States. Professional orchestras from time to time sponsor conductor competitions modeled after the prestigious European competitions.

As part of the Tanglewood Music Center's Fellowship Program, young conductors have a chance to broaden conducting experience. Under the guidance of well-known conductors, participants work with the Center's orchestra and smaller ensembles. Young conductors are chosen by audition during the winter preceding each session.

The Aspen Music Festival offers both intermediate- and advanced-level conducting classes with opportunities to perform with the student orchestra. Participants are chosen by audition.

Other opportunities for getting conducting experience are available through workshops with orchestras such as the Los Angeles Philharmonic Institute; the National Repertory Orchestra in Keystone, Colorado; the Conductor's Guild Institute and Workshops, based in West Chester, Pennsylvania; and the American Symphony Orchestra League in Washington, D.C.

ORCHESTRA ADMINISTRATION

The third professional component of an orchestra is its management. Fund-raising, youth and adult educational activities, scheduling, public relations, marketing, financial planning and budgeting, artist contracts and programming are all among the manager's duties. The degree to which the manager personally handles these jobs depends on the organization's size, but he or she is ultimately responsible for the smooth functioning of all business aspects of the symphony orchestra.

Many major orchestras maintain a full schedule for their musicians and have proportionally large administrative staffs (up to eighty people) to handle many management aspects. Each orchestra has its own organizational style, and some staff positions may not exist in all parts of the country. The following descriptions of positions with major orchestra staffs are examples of administrative careers available:

- The Chief Executive Officer (or President, Executive Director, General Manager, Managing Director, or Manager) is responsible to the orchestra's governing board for all aspects of operations, including implementation of board policies, long-range planning, contract and labor negotiations, coordination of fund-raising and ticket sales, and staff supervision. Salaries for CEOs of large orchestras are sometimes comparable to those paid to business executives in similar positions. If you would like to manage an orchestra, you must be knowledgeable about all aspects of orchestra operations: budgeting and finance, personnel relations, marketing, and law. You must combine administrative abilities with a knowledge and love of symphonic repertoire and an understanding of performance standards. Above all, you should be dedicated to the symphony orchestra field and to your own organization. Be prepared for long days of attending concerts and openings, traveling with your orchestra, and additional responsibilities, such as conducting contract negotiations.
- The Assistant Manager (or Operations Manager or Manager) assists with the management of orchestra operations, including coordinating repertoire and guest artists/conductors and overseeing administrative

9

personnel. Depending on the staff structure, the assistant manager may also be responsible for budgets and fiscal affairs, contracts and tour arrangements, and scheduling all concerts.

- The Director of Development is responsible for planning and executing annual fund-raising campaigns, preparing grant applications, and maintaining contribution records. The director of development serves as liaison between the board and fund-raising committees and may be in charge of developing endowment programs. A solid knowledge of budgeting, finance, marketing techniques, and direct mail and fund-raising psychology is essential for this job.
- The Director of Marketing and Public Relations promotes events by writing and distributing news releases to various media announcing concert dates, programs, and guest artists; arranges for feature stories about the symphony; sets up press conferences and media coverage of all special symphony events; organizes the subscription campaign; and handles such jobs as designing brochures. Duties may include preparing advertising copy as well as editing the program booklets, coordinating box office activities, handling ticket printing, developing sales reports, and supervising box office staff.
- The Director of Education works with teachers, volunteers, school administrators, and conductors in devising youth concerts and preparatory materials. The director frequently writes scripts; contracts mimes, dancers, and singers; creates activities that involve all members of the community with the orchestra; and produces adult educational programs such as preconcert lectures, recitals, and newsletters.
- The Business Manager (or Controller or Bookkeeper) prepares budgets, financial statements, and reports; and handles account payments, payroll, deposits, tax reports, and other financial matters.

Some orchestra positions do not fall within the administrative category and are often filled by musicians in addition to their regular duties as performers:

- The Librarian maintains and distributes orchestra scores and parts, purchases or rents music, and enters bowings and other markings into the parts.
- The Personnel Manager hires additional musicians as needed or finds substitutes; sees that musicians meet attendance, punctuality, and dress requirements; and ensures that management provides adequate facilities for the musicians. This position requires an individual who is fair-minded, is diplomatic, and has the respect of musicians and administrators.

- The Stage Manager sees that the stage is properly set and that back-stage facilities are ready for rehearsals and performances.

Medium-sized orchestras usually have a full-time manager, a development director, a marketing and public relations director, an accountant/bookkeeper, and other staff depending on the services the orchestra provides. Clerical help may be part-time or volunteer. Smaller orchestras often pay only the manager on a full-time basis. Most administrative work with community orchestras is handled by volunteers.

Getting Experience

A good way to get orchestra-management experience is by volunteering to work part-time or during the summer with a professional symphony orchestra. Few orchestras in the United States can afford to turn down a volunteer.

If you want to design an internship, decide which aspect of orchestra administration interests you most and write to the executive director. That person will then pass your proposal to the right person. You are more likely to be successful by being specific in your interests, rather than stating you "are willing to do anything for anyone."

Combine your college music studies with business. Bachelor of Arts programs in arts administration have been instituted at some colleges, including Miami University of Ohio and Eastern Michigan University in Ypsilanti. Graduate degrees in arts administration are conferred by Yale, the University of California at Los Angeles, and the University of Wisconsin. Harvard's Summer School Institute in Arts Management also offers a program of intensive study.

The Tanglewood Music Center in Boston has a program of volunteer internships for serious young arts-administration candidates. Through this program, interns act as the interface between the Boston Symphony management organization and the public each summer and get an overview of the operation of a major symphonic festival in the process.

Compiled with the assistance of: American Symphony Orchestra League Training Department, Aspen Music School, Association of Performing Arts Presenters, Interlochen Center for the Arts, National School Orchestra Association, Shepherd School of Music, and Tanglewood Music Center.

Armed Forces Music

The United States Army, Navy, Air Force, Marine Corps, and Coast Guard each maintain a variety of music organizations and offer career opportunities for all types of musicians. Positions are available for both men and women as vocalists, accompanists, arrangers, band members, bandmasters, music directors, music librarians, transcribers, orchestra leaders, pianists, recording technicians, instructors, and instrument-repair people.

In any branch of the service, a musician can look forward to a satisfying career, extensive travel, and financial security. Benefits include a pay scale competitive with civilian wages, as well as medical care, commissary and post-exchange privileges, and retirement pay. Even if you decide not to devote your entire career to military service, the training you receive will be excellent preparation for a civilian music career.

Requirements and opportunities vary from branch to branch, but a high level of musical skill is essential, and in all cases, auditions are held prior to enlistment. In the Army, Navy, and Air Force, recruits complete basic training then go to armed forces music training centers. (The enlistment contract for the United States Marine Band in Washington, D.C., assures that you will neither undergo Marine Corps boot camp nor be transferred from the Washington area.)

A solid working knowledge of music is a prerequisite for music organizations in all branches of the armed forces.

- Navy: Before acceptance into the Navy music program, you must demonstrate working knowledge of major or minor scales and fundamentals of music notation and terminology. You must be able to sight-read first-chair parts of standard band literature ranging from easy to moderately difficult or the second- and third-chair parts of literature ranging from moderately difficult to difficult while properly observing phrasing, dynamics, and interpretation. If accepted, you are sent to the

Armed Forces School of Music for a training course lasting twenty-three weeks. After serving full-time duty with a unit band on board a ship or on base, you may return to the Naval Music School for advanced training as a conductor, an arranger, or an instructor.

- Marine Corps: There are fourteen musical units in the United States Marine Corps: "The President's Own" United States Marine Band in Washington, D.C.; twelve Marine field bands (located in the United States and overseas); and the United States Drum and Bugle Corps. Auditions for "The President's Own" United States Marine Band and for the United States Marine Drum and Bugle Corps are held only in Washington, D.C., and applicants must travel to the audition at their own expense. Auditions for the other Marine musical units may be scheduled by contacting a local recruiter or one of the units. Musicians accepted for "The President's Own" are not required to attend basic training. All other Marine field band musicians attend basic training and then the Armed Forces School of Music. Musicians selected for the United States Marine Drum and Bugle Corps attend basic training and then report to Washington for on-site training. For more information, contact the individual units.
- Air Force: The United States Air Force Occupational Handbook lists as requirements courses in singing and ear training, piano tuning, conducting, band arranging, composition, principles of musical interpretation, and transposition. For information about Air Force bands, contact the nearest Air Force recruiter.
- Army: The Army is the largest branch of the armed forces and offers the most opportunities for musicians. The Army maintains bands in the active and reserve forces in the continental United States and abroad. Assignments can be guaranteed at the time of enlistment, ensuring the initial posting to the band of your choice. Initial contact for a career in the Army's band program is through a local recruiter who can answer your questions, arrange a personal audition, and explain special promotion opportunities. You should be a skilled performer on your instrument and have basic knowledge of music theory. Following basic training, you will be sent to the Armed Forces School of Music for a twenty-three-week music training course before assignment to your band of choice.
- Coast Guard: The Coast Guard Band's mission is to build goodwill for the Coast Guard through its performances, including concerts, ceremonies, parades, military receptions, radio and television appearances, recordings, and other performances. The forty-five-piece band often travels for a hundred days or more during the year in national "mini-

tours," and has released nineteen records and furnished concert programs for National Public Radio network. If you are accepted into the band, the Coast Guard will pay for moving and travel expenses to the Coast Guard Academy. The band makes every effort to provide each performer with a professional-quality instrument and to keep it in good repair, and each member of the Coast Guard is automatically insured under the Serviceman's Group Life Insurance. Entrance into the Coast Guard Band requires meeting not only the necessary musical standards but also all standards required for entrance into the Coast Guard. For more detailed information, contact the nearest Coast Guard recruiter prior to auditioning.

Compiled with the assistance of: United States Air Force Bands, The United States Army Band, The United States Coast Guard Band, The United States Marine Band, United States Navy Bands.

Popular Music

A tourist who asks a New York cab driver how to get to Carnegie Hall is told, "Practice, buddy, practice." The joke may be old, but the advice is sound.

If your dream is a career in popular music, be aware that the field is extremely competitive. Even if you have talent, success depends on a great deal of hard work and an even greater degree of luck. Ask most performers who have made a name for themselves in popular music about how to get started and they may tell you, "Don't." They will point out that no matter how glamorous life can be at the top, the road there gets pretty rocky and sometimes doesn't lead anywhere at all.

Ask them again, however, if they regret the struggle or would change their careers and the reply is invariably, "No." Many musicians, like artists in other fields, perform because they feel they must, because music is where their aptitude lies. They know their talent is above average; they believe they have something special to contribute or that they are good enough to make a living performing.

If that is your story, if you were born to perform and are sure you have a statement to make in popular music, then the career possibilities are many and varied. Rock, jazz, blues, country, folk, Latin, ethnic, and classical music mix and mingle in an astonishing number of ways to create the sounds of today.

You can perform solo or as part of a group and can expect to play almost anywhere: at clubs, pubs, theaters, places of worship, schools, parks, fairs, and summer festivals. You might even find yourself in a television or movie studio, working for a major record company, or performing on music videos.

And you could be playing almost any instrument: piano, guitar, synthesizer, saxophone, trumpet, and drums fit into most musical ensembles, but a mark can be made with anything from a harmonica to a sitar. Often, an unusual combination of instruments gives performing groups a uniquely appealing sound. If you have mastered more than one instrument or sing as well as play, your chances for success are that much better.

Getting Started

Don't be discouraged if your big break does not come. Plan instead on becoming one of the large number of unsung musicians who make a good, steady income doing what they love and know best: making music. It is generally from these ranks of hard-working musicians that "instant sensations" come.

To get started, you need to establish a reputation—not with the general public, but among other musicians. That means going where other musicians work. Every sizable city has a music community, but larger cities obviously offer more contacts and opportunities. The city you choose may depend on what kind of music you play or what your ultimate career goals are. Some cities are known for particular styles of music and provide unique training grounds for young musicians interested in that style. Nashville is the mecca for country and western musicians, Chicago gave birth to urban blues and is still one place to see masters of the genre in action, but you can find blues in Boston and country music in Seattle. Take advantage first of what is available close to home. Learn what you can, then move on. Experience is the key to success in this field.

If you have always wanted to work in television, your best bet is Los Angeles; New York is no longer the largest outlet for televised music.

The recording industry is centered in Los Angeles, New York, and Nashville, but important work is being done in other cities including Detroit, Chicago, and Atlanta. The center for professional musical theater is still New York, but theaters are sprouting up all over.

Most musicians working in television, theater, movies, or recording studios are session musicians, hired on a per-job basis. Some television shows have a permanent orchestra or band, but that is rare. Similarly, theaters and recording studios do not, as a rule, have house bands; when backup musicians are needed, they are drawn from a city's music community.

In any city, therefore, the same musicians turn up in any number of places. For example, a Chicago jazz trombonist leads his or her own band in a neighborhood club on Monday nights, plays in someone else's combo on Wednesday, and backs a headliner in a supper club on weekends. While evenings are devoted to live performances, days might be spent in a recording studio cutting albums or recording radio commercials. This trombonist is a successful professional musician, but does not do the same thing all the time. He or she survives in a tough profession by being good, versatile, reliable, and able to read virtually any piece of music.

Develop Skills, Versatility

To do any kind of studio work, you must be an excellent musician. There is simply no time for practice at home before a session. Studio musicians must be first-rate readers and extremely flexible. A saxophone player might have to play a musical comedy score in the morning and switch to a big band sound in the afternoon or have a record date for a country music album.

The ability to read music and the technical mastery of your instrument are minimum requirements for a performing career. To develop your skills, you should take full advantage of all the opportunities your school and community offer, such as playing in marching, concert, and dance bands; jazz and classical ensembles; orchestras; and school and church choirs. You might start your own vocal or instrumental group and donate your services to local functions such as club meetings, dinners, PTA meetings, church picnics, school dances, or private parties. The organizational and performing experience will be invaluable.

Get a college degree if at all possible. The music theory and instrumental techniques you learn will give you a solid foundation on which to build a performing repertoire.

Above all, practice! Musicians, like athletes, can only keep their working muscles in shape through constant exercise. To be a successful performing musician, you must be in top form at all times.

As basic and essential as technical skills are for a musician or entertainer, it is individual style that will make you stand out. A singer, for example, is judged on voice and training, but never those qualities alone. Intensity, sincerity, warmth, stage personality, and a special, personal way of bringing life to lyrics are what make audiences sit up and take notice. One way to develop a personal style is to learn everyone else's style to find out what has not been done.

Classical training in form, analysis, theory, and composition are important to the popular musician; harmonic knowledge and familiarity with classical technique will broaden your musical horizon. That's especially true today when so many popular composers borrow from other musical idioms in search of fresh sound combinations.

You can pick up technical skills in the classroom, but personal style can only be developed in front of an audience. You need audience reaction to know if you are on the right track. Most cities have small clubs that specialize in certain kinds of music. Find the clubs that feature your kind of music and get acquainted with the musicians.

Get to Know Other Musicians

One of the best ways for instrumentalists to break into the field is to find people who do the same thing; a trumpet player should know every other trumpet player in town. Getting to know other musicians and being accepted is necessary. Go to clubs and other performing spots with your instrument and wait for a chance to sit in on a session. Find out what places hold amateur nights. Take advantage of all chances to perform in front of an audience. Play as much as you can and practice the rest of the time. Study and play along with recordings of your favorite artists to learn their techniques.

Even after that important first break, things can be rough. Pay is minimal and bookings infrequent and uncertain. You will almost certainly need a second job. If you can find work in music education, do so; not only will you have the satisfaction of working in your field, but many school situations provide performance opportunities. Also consider a professional career in addition to music so you will have a strong alternative career if things do not work out. Even a job driving a cab or waitressing will do on a temporary basis, as long as it provides adequate financial support and leaves time for your music.

Until you are able to afford an agent or manager, you will have to find your own bookings. Build a press kit as soon as possible including personal information, photographs, and press clippings. A performance tape might also be helpful in getting a job.

When you start getting bookings, you may want to find an agent or manager. You will be spending a great deal of your time improving old material and working on new acts and will not have the time for financial, legal, and public-relations work. You should also be familiar, however, with the business aspects of performing even if someone else handles this for you.

Your life as a performer will require long hours, travel, and tough competition. But the opportunities for a successful career do exist if you are willing to work. If you believe strongly in yourself and have a mature, realistic awareness of your options, you could be one of the lucky ones.

Compiled with the assistance of: American Society of Composers, Authors, and Publishers (ASCAP) and Broadcast Music, Inc. (BMI).

CAREERS IN EDUCATION

Music Education

Music education begins at (if nor prior to) birth and carries well beyond the classroom to become a prime influence on the musical vitality of a community and the nation. Consequently, a music education career gives you an opportunity to be involved in performing and creating music and contributing to the process and pleasure of teaching music to others. It is a challenging profession, offering a large measure of personal stimulation and gratification.

Teaching Qualifications

When interviewing or being considered as a candidate for a music teaching job, in addition to the appropriate documentation (such as a bachelor's or master's degree, letters of recommendation, and college academic records), you should expect to demonstrate a number of skills or activities. According to *Music Teacher Education: Partnership and Process,* a report from the Music Educators National Conference's (MENC) Teacher Education Task Force (published in 1987 by MENC), you may be evaluated on the following skills and activities.

Instructional Skills:
- teach a lesson that illustrates knowledge of lesson planning
- conduct a rehearsal that demonstrates good rehearsal technique and preparation
- teach or conduct a lesson that demonstrates effective classroom management
- teach or conduct a lesson that illustrates knowledge of a variety of learning needs
- teach or conduct a lesson that demonstrates vocal projection, appropriate grammar, self-confidence, and general deportment

- teach or conduct a lesson that demonstrates interaction with students in asking and answering questions
- pass a state or national teacher-competency exam if required by the employing agency

Musical Skills:
- perform a composition to demonstrate musical sensitivity
- perform in a secondary medium (piano, guitar, voice, classroom or other secondary instruments) in a teaching context of the position being sought
- teach or conduct a lesson that demonstrates knowledge of music history, music theory, music composition, and creativity
- teach or conduct a lesson that demonstrates how musical listening affects musical learning
- teach or conduct a lesson that illustrates the ability to hear musical performance problems and prescribe appropriate solutions
- pass a state or national subject-matter competency exam if required by the employing agency

Personal Abilities:
- demonstrate the degree to which your professional goals have been determined
- demonstrate the nature of your commitment to teaching music
- show an understanding of the development of personal relationships with students, colleagues, administrators, parents, and community members
- demonstrate the development of a philosophy of music education

Because the ability to communicate with students is essential, music educators must have a well-developed philosophy of music and education. They should demonstrate a familiarity with contemporary educational thought and be able to apply a broad knowledge of musical repertoire to the learning problems of music students. They must be flexible and open-minded to innovation and expanding concepts. New instruments, such as synthesizers, have enlarged the musical palette, creating a need for teachers to understand not only acoustical properties of these instruments but their use in performance. As computers become more common in schools, teaching methods are changing and adapting to this technology as well.

The term "music education" covers a spectrum of specialized activities—activities that are different for each school situation or career opportunity. However, there are certain common, basic elements that may help you make a career choice.

PREKINDERGARTEN TEACHERS

Prekindergarten music education can involve children from birth to four years of age, but the most common groups served are three- and four-year-olds.

Because of the rapidly emerging need for prekindergarten music programs, today's general music teachers and music curriculum directors must understand the developmental stages of young children and be able to provide them with appropriate musical experiences. They should understand that play is the young child's way of learning. Although the young child will acquire knowledge and skills, the teacher's primary goal is the development of a positive attitude toward music.

Prekindergarten music educators should possess a high level of musicianship and be able to improvise both musically and instructionally. Although they must be able to model and guide musical experiences, they should be able to follow the child's lead, when appropriate. In addition to having empathy for very young children, they should be able to communicate effectively with them.

ELEMENTARY SCHOOL TEACHERS

Teaching music in elementary schools presents a challenging opportunity either in a full- or part-time position. Most school districts and many states have adopted specific music criteria for their schools. These include general music in which the teachers give students a broad background in musical literacy in preparation for later instruction in the performing arts. Commonly, the elementary curriculum tends to be eclectic and frequently includes approaches developed by educators such as Zoltán Kodály, Carl Orff, Emile Jaques-Dalcroze, and Shinichi Suzuki, as well as comprehensive musicianship. Often, the curriculum centers on a basal music series.

In some communities, there is a music specialist for each school responsible for most musical activities; in others, the elementary music teacher (either vocal or instrumental) may visit several schools. Some systems may have the children come to a music room, while in others the teacher goes to individual classrooms.

The instrumental teacher in a large school system may act as a specialist for instruction on strings, woodwinds, brass, or percussion. However, even these specialists are called upon to combine instruction in overlapping areas: A string teacher may do some wind or percussion instruction, or vice versa. In addition to providing instruction to beginners on various instruments, elementary instrumental teachers conduct ensembles and are responsible for promoting and developing instrumental programs.

Elementary instrumental specialists are rare in smaller schools; more common is a combined elementary general music/instrumental teacher.

In some elementary schools, class piano is offered. Often the teacher is a piano specialist. However, this responsibility may be handled by a competent general music teacher or instrumental instructor. All these positions are sometimes itinerant in nature, with teachers visiting more than one school each week, and all require the ability to communicate effectively and persuasively with different principals and numerous classroom teachers.

Any elementary music teacher should be able to play piano and guitar. He or she should have a skilled ear that will perceive pitch and interval variances so students can develop a degree of pitch discernment as well as find their singing voices. Furthermore, a teacher needs to develop a singing voice that will be an example for the children to emulate. Even more essential is a clear notion and concept of children's vocal and pitch development and of good literature.

Elementary Music Specialists

In some school systems, elementary music is taught by the classroom teacher under the guidance of a music specialist. In this case, the specialist plans and guides music learning experiences and assists the classroom teacher. This may include demonstration lessons and regularly scheduled teaching in the classroom.

In other systems, the specialist serves as a resource person, locating music materials and coordinating music activities that are integrated with school programs and academic areas. When teachers assume the role of specialist or coordinator, they also need administrative skills, since they are part of the administrative staff. Especially important is the ability to work with people.

MIDDLE OR JUNIOR HIGH SCHOOL TEACHERS

In many smaller school systems, the music teacher has a joint junior/senior high or elementary/junior high appointment, which may include a combination of vocal and instrumental music instruction. Larger systems usually have both vocal and instrumental teachers for each school.

The vocal music teacher in a middle or junior high school is normally responsible for the general music class, which provides opportunities for students to make, understand, and appreciate music, rather than stressing performance. Teachers must be prepared to instruct students in jazz, rock, folk, and popular contemporary music. Administrators and parents tend to expect accountability. Too many young people become "musical dropouts" because general music teachers lacked the imagination to make the program meaningful; thus, the teacher needs to exercise creativity.

SENIOR HIGH SCHOOL TEACHERS

In smaller communities, the senior high school music teacher may also work in a junior high or elementary school. However, where there is a large enough enrollment in the senior high school, the music teacher usually functions in a single school as a resident vocal or instrumental teacher.

Occasionally, where the school population is too small to support a single teacher in both fields or where it may be so large that it requires three or four teachers, assignments may overlap. An instrumentalist might teach general music or vocal class; a vocalist with an instrumental proficiency might handle a single instrumental section. In systems with declining enrollment, a music specialist may be called on to teach other subjects as well. In large senior high schools with several music staff members, teachers are usually band, orchestra, or choral directors. These schools may expect some prior, successful teaching experience from job applicants.

Senior high school music electives include theory, music appreciation, history and literature, general music, music in combination with other arts (for example, a related arts course), voice classes, and small ensembles. Staff members are assigned to these courses according to their training and experience.

The voice specialist in most senior high schools should have voice training and some choral conducting experience. The ability to play piano is required for accompaniments when coaching voice or when an accompanist is not available for rehearsals. Many high schools have a mixed choir or separate boys' and girls' choruses, all of which may come under the direction of the choral music teacher.

INSTRUMENTAL MUSIC

Because no band or orchestra director can rely on students automatically participating in music, instrumental teachers must be able to recruit and instruct beginning talent. They may also teach in lower grades to help encourage a continuous supply of instrumental students. It is not unusual to find orchestra and band directors teaching beginning classes in elementary or junior high schools. Knowledge of scheduling and ability to persuade and to compromise become critically important. The music teacher, perhaps second only to the principal, must develop insight into the total district, the school schedule, and counseling as well.

In most situations, the instrumental teacher must be equipped to teach wind, string, and percussion instruments, although some school systems may have specialists in these areas. Most schools offer both orchestra and band programs, and it is necessary for instrumental teachers to be able to train and conduct such ensembles. Instrumental instructors also should be prepared to teach jazz programs, which have become more and more a part of the regular curriculum.

MUSIC SUPERVISORS IN SCHOOL SYSTEMS

In large communities where there is a staffing hierarchy, the supervision of classroom instruction is often a responsibility of supervisors. These individuals spend most of their time in the schools working with teachers and students. They demonstrate teaching techniques, provide in-service training courses for classroom teachers, evaluate instruction, and coordinate large district or city programs.

A music supervisor or director should enjoy working with both adults and children and have a personality that instills confidence and elicits cooperation from the staff. He or she also should possess a level of musical ability that commands the respect of the community's musicians. With these qualities, a supervisor will enhance the overall position of music in the school system.

COLLEGE TEACHERS

Teaching at the college level requires basic competencies beyond undergraduate preparation; in most cases, beyond completion of a master's degree, approaching the completion of a doctorate. If candidates have developed performance skills along with an international reputation, an appointment as an artist faculty member is possible.

In today's academic market, a prospective college teacher must have a Master of Music, Master of Fine Arts, doctorate, or doctorate in progress. The content of these degrees is expected to match the qualifications of the position being sought. College teaching appointments vary according to the size of the department, school, or college of music. Music education professors may teach all aspects of a music education undergraduate curriculum and some or all graduate classes. Student teaching and intern observation is usually a part of the faculty load.

A college music faculty member must have excellent performing, writing, and organizational skills. All faculty are required to demonstrate advanced musical skills in a variety of settings, to write for publication in a refereed journal, and to participate in many committee activities requiring verbal and written communication skills.

The faculty member whose primary appointment is in applied music must give regular recitals, write for publication in a relevant music journal, and actively participate in recruitment. If the appointment includes ensemble work, there is usually a required minimum of two concerts a year. College music teaching is intensely demanding, yet it is very satisfying as a professional career.

STATE SUPERVISORS OF MUSIC

The number of state supervisors of music has increased, although supervision of combined arts is taking the place of the focused music person in some states. With this increase in number, the role of state supervisor of music education has taken on added significance.

State supervisors serve as resource and staff personnel to state departments of education which, in turn, make recommendations to state legislatures and state boards of education. State supervisors of music also serve as liaisons between disciplines, helping coordinate music with other subject fields in curricular matters. They take the lead in setting standards for classroom instruction; enforcing, designing, and implementing curricula; and evaluating programs and students.

When selecting state supervisors of music, committees usually seek individuals with years of successful teaching experience in a variety of situations, preferably at all grade levels and in both vocal and instrumental music. Because these positions are dependent upon funds allocated by state legislatures, state supervisors do not always receive a salary commensurate with their experience and responsibilities.

As in any administrative position, state music supervisors must possess skills in working with people, be convincing in their knowledge of the subject, and be capable of inspiring both laypersons and music teachers in order to strengthen the integral role of music in education. They should be skilled musicians and teachers, have a broad cultural background, and be able to see music as part of the total educational experience.

The state supervisor of music keeps music teachers informed of current developments in music education, is available for consultation, and gives advice about expanding music programs and improving instruction.

Training for Music Education

In the United States, there is no central agency for licensing teachers. Each state sets its own requirements and issues necessary licenses to teach within its borders. However, there is general agreement among states on qualifications and a great deal of reciprocity. You should check with the appropriate state department of education for information about licensing or certification requirements. The music education department at any college or university also may help you in determining certification requirements for a specific state.

The prospective teacher has the responsibility to expand experiences and understandings beyond the discipline chosen for a career. Music education students must grow intellectually through the study of liberal arts and sciences that constitute our broad cultural heritage. Through these experiences, students develop resources, understandings, and personal skills from which to draw for future growth. The diversity of such experiences allows the student to struggle with new models for thinking—in both traditional and developing disciplines. Furthermore, it can foster the development of intelligent decisions regarding the role of music in our society and in making judgments about the quality of musical literature and performance. Therefore, intellectually, the music teacher should:

- expand personal curiosity for learning itself—not confined to a specific discipline
- discover new intellectual resources that challenge traditional viewpoints
- apply the skills of critical thinking to daily problem solving
- investigate the use and value of music in various societies
- develop an understanding of the related arts and various theories of aesthetic meaning
- seek to understand and respect diversity in individuals and ideas

Most music students enter college with a considerable background in musical performance. The college program expands those experiences by providing formal coursework for the acquisition of musical knowledge and the development of personal skills as the student makes a mature commitment to the profession. Through the process of becoming familiar with one's musical performance, creativity, and understanding, the prospective music teacher must learn to see how all musical experiences combine as preparation for teaching.

The applied lessons, classes, and performing ensembles provide model settings through which understanding of performance problems, active listening, musical analysis, rehearsal design, conducting, and class planning are observed and evaluated. Through these daily contacts, ideas and techniques for teaching music are perceived and reinforced. From a musical growth aspect, the prospective music teacher should:

- demonstrate skill in listening, analyzing, notating, arranging, composing, improvising, performing, rehearsing, and evaluating
- understand the broad relationships among musical styles, musical forms, historical periods, and composers
- investigate the artistic and sociopolitical influences found in the music that is studied
- apply qualitative criteria in making judgments about the music selected for study and performance
- develop analytical procedures based on an aural perception of music to go beyond sets of rules and non–sound-oriented techniques
- utilize technology to practice and develop ear training, sight singing, and other skills that translate notation into music in an accurate and artistic fashion
- integrate the understandings gained from his or her training (including music history, theory, performance, and creative activities) into the providing of musical experiences for all music classes (including solo, chamber, and large-ensemble performance classes) and in determining performance practice
- develop creative skills for use in performance
- develop sight-reading skills to learn new music quickly, accompany others, and transpose music for classroom use
- demonstrate knowledge of instrumental or vocal pedagogy and performance practice by modeling on piano, voice, fretted classroom instruments, and secondary instruments
- detect errors in performance and demonstrate the correct response

Most music students require the expertise and assistance of a well-prepared teacher if they are to understand and demonstrate personal mastery of a subject. Some students may learn regardless of the quality of the guidance; most, however, benefit from systematic and insightful leadership. Formal courses in education and special methods courses in music education must assist the teacher candidate in developing the myriad skills and knowledge that can help students learn music. Formal coursework must be matched with opportunities for practical application of theories and good principles of instruction. The process of learning how to teach should place the prospective teacher in a variety of teaching/learning settings throughout the teacher certification program. As a prospective music teacher, while in college you can expect to:

- demonstrate understanding of the theories of sensation, attention, perception, growth and development, motivation, and other aspects of human behavior

- apply knowledge regarding the cognitive, affective, and psychomotor domains of learning to instruction planning
- seek answers to instructional problems from appropriate research
- explore the use of personal, intellectual, musical, and instructional resources in peer and small-group instruction and in on-site classroom and rehearsal observations
- perceive and evaluate evidence of unique learning styles and varied stages and levels of learning as they are observed in field experience
- develop the capacity to make intelligent decisions for sequencing instruction: (1) prepare program objectives, (2) write objectives that can be implemented and evaluated, (3) describe learning outcomes for short- and long-term instruction, (4) prepare learning objectives in a logical and systematic sequence, and (5) accommodate a wide range of special learning needs and musical backgrounds
- demonstrate a practical understanding of a variety of teaching techniques and methodologies: (1) determine the most effective technique for a given setting and student, (2) facilitate the interest and needs of individual students within a large class, and (3) design and teach individual and small-group activities that enrich curricular goals and provide remedial work for those students who need additional reinforcement
- develop understanding of effective evaluation of learning and teaching
- demonstrate effective skills in written, spoken, and musical communication
- develop an understanding of the philosophical viewpoints regarding value in the disciplines of music education
- employ educational technology in a manner that enhances the effectiveness of learning for individual students

Finding a Job

The more specific you are about the field of music you wish to teach, the more flexible you must be with respect to where you are willing to teach. The nature of the job market varies considerably from state to state and even within states. Any capable teacher who is willing to work in a geographic area that has a shortage of teachers (such as inner cities or rural communities) will probably find a job.

If you are seeking employment in areas where there are special considerations or problems, you must not only be knowledgeable in your subject but able to cope with unusual situations. You should have some background in sociology and psychology. It is especially desirable that you do your student teaching where similar conditions prevail.

If you want a job in a particular part of the country, apply through school district personnel offices in surrounding communities as well as in the specific location. Nearly all universities have placement bureaus, and while these agencies are effective, you should not rely on them entirely. Other resources include your college's music education faculty, some state music associations, and the Music Educators National Conference.

Interviewing for a Position

If you want to conduct choirs exclusively, keep in mind that there are few such assignments. Most vocal teachers work in related fields such as general music, voice classes, theory, or even other subject areas. Instrumental assignments in senior high schools often involve a combination of theory, music appreciation, and other subjects.

It is important to remember that the perfect job does not exist. When applying for a position, you must be prepared to assume obligations that may not always be at the top of your priority list.

Most interviewers are interested in how you think and your musical abilities. Be prepared to perform in order to demonstrate your musicality.

Usually the focus of the interview or audition is based on the job being filled. For example, for an elementary school job you might be asked to play a simple song accompaniment on piano or guitar. Applying for a senior high school orchestra position may require performing on your major instrument or conducting. It is not out of line to ask beforehand about the nature of the audition/interview if one is required. Interviews not only help the employer learn more about you, but they also help you learn about the position.

Compiled with the assistance of: The College Music Society and Music Educators National Conference. Special thanks to Barbara Andress for the section on prekindergarten teachers and to Irma Collins for the section on college teachers.

Independent Teaching

If you are interested in teaching music, working in a school setting is not your only option. You may want to give some thought to going into business for yourself.

Well-qualified, dedicated, independent music teachers are in demand in many geographic areas. As an independent teacher, you will have the satisfaction of sharing your vocal or instrumental music mastery with others and of being your own boss.

Independent teaching is flexible; it can be a full-time career or a part-time means of supplementing income. You plan your own schedule, so your work week can be as long or as short as you like. You can work out of your home or rent a studio in another location, such as a small retail store.

Many music stores have instrumental or voice instruction programs that employ independent teachers. In some cases, the teachers are salaried employees, either full- or part-time, who also serve on the sales staff or as teaching program coordinators. In other instances, teachers may rent studio space from the store and collect fees themselves from the students; some use in-store space free of charge.

Opportunities as a full-time independent teacher vary from place to place. Many areas of the country with few or no school music programs have strong demand for lessons. In communities with strong school band, orchestra, and choral programs, the number of students involved often prevents the director from giving students individual attention. Lessons on a one-to-one basis can be a valuable supplement to school programs. However, check out the competition in the area; your specialty may already be taught by several others.

The greatest demand is for piano, organ, and guitar teachers. These are the most popular instruments among America's amateur musicians and are not taught as part of the school music curriculum as often as band and orchestral instruments.

Parents who want to introduce children to music often begin with piano because lessons can be started at an earlier age than for most other instruments. Especially among teenagers and young adults, interest in the guitar is strong, and qualified teachers have little trouble attracting students. Recent trends have shown that many adults who wish to develop proficiency on an instrument or to increase the training they acquired as children are taking lessons. This group includes some of the most dedicated and interested students and now constitutes a large and growing market.

Many independent teachers explore group instructional methods, which are especially applicable to teaching piano and guitar. For some teachers, group instruction is more challenging and better paying than one-on-one teaching. Before entering a group teaching situation, investigate the large number of commercially available lesson programs and curricula. You may want to use an existing method or create your own. Group guitar lessons can easily be organized in your own home; all you need is a well-lighted space, a blackboard, and some folding chairs. Group piano requires more than one instrument and is most conveniently taught in a studio situation.

Many programs combine the best attributes of both private and group lessons into a curriculum that provides total musicianship, including performance skills, theory, ear training, improvising, and composing. Also, independent teachers are exploring the incorporation of modern technology—computer-assisted instruction, synthesizers, electronic keyboards—into their instructional programs.

The profession of independent teaching is flexible and self-regulating in terms of size of class, kind of students, type of studio, and size of income. This fact should not in any way detract from the necessity of full- and part-time independent teachers to continue to grow and work toward the highest educational, pedagogical, and musical credentials they can attain and the most businesslike decorum for their studios.

Training

To succeed as an independent music teacher, you must give attention to your musical, educational, and pedagogical development. Get the best training possible. Many colleges offer courses and degrees in pedagogy as a valuable background for independent teachers. The more versatile you are, the better your chances of success. Know the capabilities of your instrument or voice and be able to demonstrate them. A degree in music from a college or conservatory is desirable, but extensive performing experience may be substituted if you are open to the requirements of teaching.

In addition to being a good musician and keeping musically active, you must have an aptitude for and desire to teach. You will need patience and an ability to accomplish musical objectives quickly and successfully. Some of the prerequisites of independent teaching include:

- knowledge of child (and general human) development, stages of learning, and learning styles
- a broad knowledge of teaching material and repertoire available for the level(s) of students you wish to teach
- a broad-based (and open-minded) musical knowledge, including music history, stylistic considerations, compositional techniques, and theory
- an ability to communicate in a concise, understandable fashion and an excellent verbal and written command of the language
- a reasonable proficiency in playing many types of music and in sight-reading
- an ability to adjust teaching style to the needs of the individual student

Being able to generate enthusiasm as you teach is essential. Join professional music organizations so you can associate with your fellow teachers. Attend workshops and clinics and subscribe to professional journals to keep informed about new teaching methods and materials.

An independent teacher is really a small-business owner. Conducting your studio in a businesslike manner, keeping records for tax purposes, and making wise decisions about equipment and materials are part of successful studio teaching.

To be a good teacher, you must enjoy teaching and the creative process of helping your students grow as musicians. Good teachers always remain students themselves, searching constantly for ways to improve their teaching and keep ahead of new developments in their field.

Compiled with the assistance of: Music Educators National Conference, Music Teachers National Association, and American String Teachers Association.

Band Directing

There are few careers that offer the personal and professional satisfaction found in band directing if the director brings to the job two essential characteristics: love of music and love of people.

For those who truly love music, the career possibilities as a band director are extensive. If you are considering band directing as a profession, music should be such an important part of your life that sharing this enthusiasm is your motivation for becoming a conductor/teacher. As a teacher, and all directors are teachers, you become a model for your students. You will be setting out to infect them with that wonderful "musical disease" for which there is no known cure! What better career motivation than adding the exciting dimension of music to other people's lives?

The second characteristic a successful band conductor/teacher must have is love of people. Your effect as a teacher of music, again as a model, must reflect your enthusiasm and concern for your students as performers and as individuals. If you possess, as one eminent band director described, these "passions" for music and people, you have the two characteristics that identify the truly successful, productive, and sustaining professional.

If you plan to pursue a band directing career, you should play an instrument with a sufficient degree of competence so that expressive performance is second nature. A correspondent facility on the piano and comfortable command of singing also are assets that reinforce musical awareness. These assets should be developed as part of your college preparation.

Band directing is a multifaceted occupation. If you find variety attractive and stimulating, the band directing profession will continue to provide interesting experiences throughout your career.

Directing a band provides opportunities for interacting with many different types of people in many social and professional situations. It involves you in a variety of activities and enables you to develop musical skills and perceptions as a performer, a teacher of instruments, and a composer/arranger. You will acquire administrative abilities and become a leader in your school and community, since the band director is undeniably visible.

Educational Requirements

The types of bands in which you can pursue your career are nearly as varied as the job itself: elementary school, middle/junior high school, senior high school, junior/community college, college/university, military, professional, and community.

In addition, if you are a member of a drum and bugle corps, there may be a place for you as an independent instructor when you leave the corps. Drum corps often have several part-time teachers in specialized areas such as drilling and color guard choreography, brass, and percussion techniques.

The corps may pay a small fee for part-time teachers during winter practice season and a larger stipend during the busy summer competition period. Teachers usually travel with the corps during the summer with all expenses paid.

A bachelor's degree in music or music education is required for virtually all these positions, with the exception of a few community bands. This degree includes, among other studies, a professional sequence of courses in music theory, history, conducting, methodology, psychology, and applied music. Degrees in music education prepare you for a practical internship in the schools, supervised by an experienced teacher, and lead to teacher certification. The Bachelor of Music degree concentrates on music and does not include educational theory, methodology, or practice. The culmination of this degree is a series of professional recitals. Although you can include a conducting emphasis with this degree, it does not prepare you for certification in music education.

Graduate degrees in performance, conducting, composition, history, or related musical subjects (some of which exclude education curricula) may open doors for conducting opportunities at colleges or universities, in military or service bands, or in professional or community bands. It should be noted that military bands have their own courses of study that prepare their conductors for responsibilities unique to military functions. Virtually all college or university positions require a master's degree or professional equivalent and, more often than not, a doctoral degree of some kind.

Opportunities for Women

Although band directing was once considered a "man's world," directing opportunities available to women are now nearly on a par with those for men. There are not as many women holding positions of professional eminence in high school, college, or professional ranks. There are, however, women in each of these areas who have brought themselves distinction and provided splendid models for others interested in band directing.

Each of the directing positions, ranging from elementary band instructor to director of professional ensembles, requires unique qualities.

A well-prepared conductor/teacher will be able to work with any of the designated age-groups. However, there are those directors who find great rewards in teaching young students, focusing on teaching fundamentals, and getting the satisfaction that comes from providing a sound foundation on which subsequent progress will be based. Others find the channeling of preadolescent energy not only challenging but thoroughly satisfying. Still other directors enjoy the program variety and activity schedule that characterizes high school band directing.

The high school years are also a period in which technical and musical achievements can complement directing interests with even more challenging and sophisticated literature. College or university positions often are assumed by high school directors who have developed outstanding programs and are anxious to work with even more mature performers and challenging literature. Teachers prepare for these higher education positions through graduate study and by challenging their high school bands to performance standards that bring these ensembles to the attention of the professional community.

The Future of Band Directing

The future of band directing is encouraging. As more students enter college, there will be a correspondent opportunity there. The rapidly growing community band movement, as well as opportunities in military bands for performers and directors, provide even more positions for conductors.

Where do you find out more about these opportunities? First contact the chairman, director, or dean of the school or department of music that most interests you. Do not limit yourself to one school. Ask music teachers whose work you admire and your school guidance counselors to suggest good schools. There are schools known and highly regarded for their teacher education programs, some for outstanding graduate or undergraduate programs and others for their comprehensiveness. Do everything you can to attend a school that has the staff, ensembles, and facilities to challenge you and provide comprehensive preparation.

Recommended Preparation

In preparing for a career in band directing, it will be to your advantage to develop performing skills to the highest degree. If you can take a music

41

theory course in senior high school, it is always beneficial. If time and your schedule permit, do everything you can to get choral and instrumental experiences.

Finally, a leadership role in your band or orchestra is particularly good preparation. Work as a director's student assistant, gather experience and ask questions, start reading professional magazines and journals, and become familiar with professional music education organizations and the role these groups can play in your development. Help your director with charting halftime shows, direct the pep band, coach your own ensemble. The possibilities for getting experience are almost limitless; be assured, busy band directors seldom turn down volunteers who are seriously considering the profession.

Compiled with the assistance of: College Band Directors National Association, Women Band Directors National Association, and National Band Association.

CAREERS
IN BUSINESS

Retailing

If you play a musical instrument, it more than likely came from one of the thousands of retail stores that employ people in every capacity from manager to teacher to instrument-repair specialist. While there are retail chains with music stores in several states, most owners operate just one or two stores and get involved in every aspect of their business.

There are four main types of music retailers:

- the full-line dealer who carries all types of instruments and musical accessories
- the school music dealer who specializes in band and orchestra instruments and amplification equipment
- the keyboard dealer who concentrates on pianos, organs, synthesizers, and electronic keyboards and generally travels from school to school calling on educators
- the combo/sound reinforcement dealer who sells primarily amplifiers, guitars, electronic keyboards, and synthesizers

While the majority of musical instruments and accessories are sold through music retailers, some instruments, such as portable keyboards, are sold by department stores and mass merchandisers. A variety of sound reinforcement equipment is also available through audio stores. Many retailers also have flourishing instructional programs that require in-store space and a sizable teaching staff.

Regardless of the retailer's specialty (such as providing a teaching studio) or depth of music he or she provides, the basic skill required in retailing is the ability to sell. With increasing new technology, product knowledge is also extremely important, especially in combo instrument sales.

Opportunities and Professional Qualifications

Anyone with a gift for persuasion and sense of conviction can sell. But in a music store, you will be in a better position to counsel the customer if you can play an instrument.

And, because retailing is becoming increasingly complex, more and more music store managers also want employees with college degrees. When checking into a school that offers a degree in music business, be aware that some business degree programs include recording (that is, operating or owning a sound/recording studio), while others are for arts management. Should you desire a career in music retailing, pursue a degree that will assist you in those areas. Many colleges now offer a combined music/business degree program for musically oriented people who want to pursue nonperformance careers.

Some colleges with good programs in this subject area are: Appalachian State University, Boone, North Carolina; Bradley University, Peoria, Illinois; Clarion University, Clarion, Pennsylvania; University of Colorado, Denver; Crane School of Music of the State University of New York at Potsdam; Eastern Kentucky University, Richmond; Elmhurst College, Elmhurst, Illinois; University of Evansville, Evansville, Indiana; Florida Southern College, Lakeland; Hofstra University, Hempstead, New York; Indiana State University, Terre Haute; Kearney State College, Kearney, Nebraska; James Madison University, Harrisonburg, Virginia; University of Miami, Coral Gables, Florida; Millersville University, Millersville, Pennsylvania; Northeast Missouri State University, Kirksville; Red Deer College, Red Deer, Alberta, Canada; South Dakota State University, Brookings; University of Southern Mississippi, Hattiesburg; Southwestern Oklahoma State University, Weatherford; State University of New York College at Fredonia; University of Texas, San Antonio; Valparaiso University, Valparaiso, Indiana; West Virginia Institute of Technology, Montgomery; Western Illinois University, Macomb; Wingate College, Wingate, North Carolina; and University of Wisconsin—Oshkosh.

Many larger music retail stores (usually those in the full-line category) offer internships or work-study programs for students enrolled in joint degree programs at area colleges and universities. Smaller retailers may have entry-level openings for students without college training who have deep interest and performing proficiency in music. If you are considering music retailing, however, be realistic about the possibilities for advancement to a management position without a college degree, especially if you have competition from employees with business administration courses or degrees. If you cannot afford to attend college full-time, you should consider evening courses in business and retailing to augment your interest in the music field.

Many music retailers looking for college-trained employees rely on recommendations from music educators at area colleges and universities. Top managers of large, multistore operations often recruit on college campuses across the country for their beginning management and sales personnel. However, the non–college-trained person with an interest in music can usually explore job opportunities by establishing personal contact with local music retailers.

What's in It for You?

Annual salaries for music store salespeople vary depending upon the person's ability and motivation and the reputation of the store for which he or she works. Store location, brands of instruments the store carries, and the promotion, advertising, and public relations support by the store owner and manufacturer also influence the earnings of the sales staff.

Many pay plans are available, including straight commission, combined salary and commission, or straight salary. (For current information about salary and types of payment, contact the National Association of Music Merchants [NAMM] in Carlsbad, California, for a copy of its Compensation and Benefits Study.)

Where Do You Fit in?

Depending on the type of music store in which you plan to work, you may sell pianos, electronic keyboards, sound reinforcement equipment, wind instruments, or even accessories. You will fit in with the store management and other salespeople if you share their interest in music and their conviction that they are selling a valued commodity, music and its enjoyment, to their customers.

NAMM also has available a series of cassette tapes, "The Business of Music," which covers a variety of selling approaches and problems, as well as sales training videotapes titled "Success on Your Terms." NAMM also has a complete library of sales training materials that provides a variety of information. If you want a head start on your selling career while still a student, check with your school's music department or library (since many colleges offering joint business/music degrees have these tapes in their libraries) or contact NAMM directly.

MUSIC STORE TEACHING

Many large music stores have extensive studio teaching operations, often managed by an educational director who is an authority in the music education field. In many cases, the educational director is also the store's contact with music teachers in private studios, public and parochial elementary and secondary schools, area colleges, and conservatories. This person is usually the primary teacher at the store.

The in-store educational director usually has at least a bachelor's degree in music education (preferably a master's degree) and teaching experience. This background makes the director the professional equal of the teachers who are customers and tends to attract these people to the store.

The educational director arranges store recitals, oversees educational operations, and often leads workshops for music teachers. The director may also initiate in-school, group-instruction programs (working with local faculty members), arrange band and orchestra competitions, work with community band programs, and engage in public relations efforts that promote store sales, as well as teach.

BECOMING A SALES MANAGER

In a large full-line music store, there are managers for each department who supervise sales personnel and take part in the general operation of the store. Sales managers usually rise from the ranks of sales personnel after proving their abilities. Age and seniority are not the only criteria for advancement. Extensive knowledge of a particular product area (such as guitars and amplifiers) can help a young person advance more quickly to a supervisory post. Sales managers also order merchandise, evaluate inventory and turnover, and set performance standards and sales quotas for all personnel.

Retailers that operate more than one outlet usually choose outstanding sales managers to run the individual stores. Again, the criteria for advancement to store manager are administrative and sales ability and solid background and experience in the business skills needed to run a retail store for maximum profit.

In medium- and large-sized music retail outlets, other management opportunities may include being a department or division manager, such as in the sheet music, repair and service, shipping, accessories, or instrument rental departments.

OPPORTUNITIES IN SERVICE AND REPAIRS

There are many job opportunities available in the area of musical instrument repair and service. One area is the repair and service of acoustic instruments, which is usually done at independent shops or in the repair/service department of a music retail store. Electronic instrument repair and service will require a more technical background. If your inter-

48

ests lie in either of these areas, you should check with various service/repair organizations, such as the Piano Technicians Guild, for additional information.

STARTING YOUR OWN MUSIC STORE

The person who establishes a retail store generally has experience selling musical instruments, accessories, and supplies. A store owner should be well trained in business administration, merchandising, advertising and promotion, sales, and personnel management. Most successful music retailers have risen through the ranks and have combined a college degree in business or music with an inherent love of music and practical selling experience.

The major requisites for a successful music store owner are:

- sufficient capital backing and source of financing
- good store location in the right market
- business acumen, sensitivity to people, and solid educational background in business administration and music
- administrative ability and management skills
- demonstrated salesmanship
- ability to play an instrument and interest in music performance
- interest in music education; knowing the latest trends at all levels of school music instruction, as well as teaching approaches and programs of major manufacturers and manufacturers' associations
- good personal and professional relationships and rapport with independent and group teachers, school music personnel, and college music faculty members, as well as church and civic personnel
- strong sense of public and community relations; true involvement in the community

Successful music retailers never really stop selling even when they can afford to hire all the sales personnel they need. They stay active in professional associations, educator groups, and civic and business organizations at the local, state, and national levels. (NAMM also has available a variety of manuals on topics such as managing/starting a business, credit and collections, and personnel, which may be of interest to the prospective music retailer.)

Compiled with the assistance of: National Association of Music Merchants.

Distributing

For the business-minded music student who likes selling but does not want to go into retailing, distribution offers another challenging career possibility.

The distributor, the liaison between manufacturer and retailer, buys and warehouses many types of instruments, sheet music, and accessories and resells to music retailers who may want anything from a single bass guitar or a gross of self-instruction aids to a dozen violin strings or a thousand harmonicas. Distributors supply large and small music retailers. They also import instruments in quantities large enough to make them competitively priced for consumer resale.

As in most businesses, distributors have salespeople assigned to specific territories, which might encompass several states with hundreds of retailers. Salespeople visit retailers on a regular basis, providing advice on best-selling products and merchandising techniques, displaying new products, and taking orders.

Some distributors also manufacture small instruments in their own facilities or may be the exclusive importers of instruments manufactured abroad to their own specifications and under their own names.

In addition, there are opportunities in the distribution area for advertising specialists, including artists and copywriters. Many distributors also have their own repair and maintenance service staffs as well as personnel in charge of stock, packing and shipping, and taking orders. Some distributors who do not have their own service staff have access to people in their communities who can do the necessary repairs.

Salaries for the various job classifications are about equal to those for similar jobs in other industries in the distributing area. Pay scales for the sales staff tend to be somewhat higher than those in retail sales but depend on the abilities of the individual salesperson, size of the territory, and number of retailers serviced.

Educational requirements also match those for similar jobs in other industries. While distributors do not need to play an instrument well, they should know the products they sell, their capabilities, and their limitations.

Compiled with the assistance of: Music Distributors Association and National Association of Music Merchants.

Manufacturing

Job opportunities in music manufacturing have grown over the years as increased interest in making music has swelled the ranks of amateurs and the demand for all types of instruments. The most recent and extremely popular additions have been instruments that require electronic circuitry, such as synthesizers.

THE PRODUCTION STAFF

For centuries, the production of musical instruments was the work of skilled artisans who carefully handcrafted and assembled the various pieces. Some of the handcrafting aspects of manufacturing have been changed by technological advances in the past fifty years, and assembly-line methods and new materials and technologies, such as plastics and electronics, have greatly affected the industry.

Different skills are required for the manufacture of different instruments. There is a need in all phases, however, for tool and die makers, assemblers, screw machine operators, buffers, sanders, and tuners. Manufacturers of brass and some woodwind instruments have positions for die casters, solderers, engravers, lacquerers, platers, valve makers, and others skilled in assembling various elements as the instruments near completion.

The newer instruments, such as synthesizers, require the talents of engineers who understand microcircuitry and computer technology. Since electronic instruments contain chips to handle a variety of functions, engineers must understand not only the functions of the components but their musical potential as well.

Pianos, despite changes in style and appearance, are basically the same instruments they have always been. Modern production methods may be used to manufacture metal interior pieces and for primary woodworking, veneering, and mill operations, but the final product is the result of handcrafting and skilled artisanship.

53

Likewise, there are few shortcuts in the manufacture of quality guitars, violins, and other stringed instruments. Highly refined woodworking skills are necessary for the production of a good stringed instrument and its decorative carving or inlay.

Among traditional musical instruments, drums have perhaps benefited most from the development of new materials. Plastics have replaced animal skins as drumheads and are widely used for the bodies. The finished drum, however, still requires handwork. Skilled craftsmanship is necessary for gluing joints, centering the head, trimming, sanding, and tuning. The final assembly of any instrument, in fact, is reserved for the best trained and most highly skilled members of the production staff.

After completion, each instrument is evaluated by a tester before it leaves the plant. Testers must be musicians as well as craftsmen, familiar with the instrument and its musical capabilities and able to make minor adjustments or pinpoint problems for adjustment by others on the production line.

While some production functions can be handled by a person without musical training, knowing how to play the instrument is an important asset. According to one manufacturer, knowing how to play an instrument might be compared to having a college degree in another field. In many instances it will be helpful in progressing to a more skilled, better paying job.

If you are interested in a career in musical instrument manufacturing, you can find job opportunities around the United States. The supply industries, those making cast-iron plates, actions, keyboards, hardware, tuning pins, strings, and mouthpieces are generally located near the manufacturing site.

For a career in instrument manufacturing, you must meet age requirements of various states as well as labor and insurance laws. You do not need any basic skills for a beginning job other than the ability to learn, since most manufacturers have on-the-job training programs. Some firms also have apprenticeship programs for the more skilled craft jobs.

A workweek generally consists of five eight-hour days with overtime pay for more than forty hours of work. This may vary, since some companies work longer hours during the production season but close the plant for a month-long summer vacation.

In most organizations, production management personnel are recruited from the ranks of experienced and skilled production staff. Management-level personnel can often, however, move to other companies in the industry or even to management jobs in completely different fields.

INVENTORS

Another possibility for a career in instrument manufacturing lies in design and development. Often, specialists in other fields, such as electronics and engineering, computer software, or music performance, have created new instruments that have led to the development of new industries.

Influential musical instrument inventors have included John Philip Sousa, sousaphone; Laurens Hammond, electric organ; Harold Rhodes, electric piano; Robert Moog and RCA engineers Harry Olson and Herbert Belar, synthesizer; and John Chowning of Stanford University, digital synthesizer. Hundreds of others have made refinements in basic instruments or created accessory items, amplification equipment, and adapters that have broadened the capabilities of instruments or have made them easier to play.

SALES REPRESENTATIVES

After manufacture, instruments can be sold directly to retail music stores or handled through jobbers, wholesalers, or distributors.

Most manufacturers have a field organization of sales representatives who are strategically located throughout the country and responsible for particular territories. Some companies use the services of manufacturers' representatives who handle several brand names.

To become a sales representative, you must know your product and establish good business relations with music retailers in your area. The job requires knowledge of retail sales, advertising, store display, retail personnel relations, and credit and collections, and an up-to-the-minute familiarity with the market and competitive conditions. You must be a self-starter, dependable, and able to communicate; you need not play an instrument.

Compensation is usually good, and is related to dollar volume of sales by territory. It is paid in the form of salary plus reimbursed expenses, commission and expenses, or a combination of both.

Sales representatives may report to a regional field representative, but they often work directly with the company sales manager, who is located at or near company headquarters. The sales manager, using product and market studies and statistics developed from company and industry experience as well as outside mercantile information, must project instrument requirements for months ahead to be used as a production guide.

Overall, the sales manager plans and carries out all company sales meetings, hires and trains salespeople, arranges and sometimes attends dealer meetings, and takes care of all details related to the sales staff.

THE MARKETING STAFF

The combination of sales, advertising, and promotion is collectively called marketing.

A marketing manager or director has overall responsibility for developing and coordinating a long-range marketing plan. This person can be involved with product development, support materials (such as owner's manuals), forecasting production and product mix, new product introduction, and more.

The advertising manager prepares an advertising budget, usually for a twelve-month fiscal period, then uses available funds in the most effective manner. The ad manager also is responsible for materials used by music retailers to describe the products to their customers: these may include catalogs, folders, specifications, service and operating manuals, banners, and signs. The ad manager supervises all advertising in newspapers, educational journals, and magazines, and on radio and television.

Some companies maintain a complete advertising department and are equipped to handle all in-house requirements. Most, however, have limited staff and use independent advertising agencies for creative talent and service assistance. As an adjunct of the advertising department, a few companies maintain a program of public relations.

OTHER MANUFACTURING PERSONNEL

Product specialists assist sales managers in demonstrations, educate salespeople and music retailers, and study the field directly related to the products for which they are responsible. They monitor and become the resident experts on all competitive products.

Artist relations is an area that also can be very stimulating. The artist relations specialist is a person who works with professional musicians to explore ideas for new musical products and uses the pros in advertising campaigns.

Especially important to a manufacturing plant is the service department, staffed by experts thoroughly familiar with the product. The service staff handles any problems with product, gives advice and instruction, and sends replacement parts when needed. Staffers deal with retailers, jobbers, wholesalers, distributors, independent technicians, and owners of both old and new instruments.

The musical instrument manufacturing industry, like any other business, relies on a number of other departments to make operations run smoothly. These include personnel, purchasing, payroll, credit, and accounting.

Educational requirements for the various jobs described in this chapter vary according to individual responsibilities. Generally, a high school degree is necessary for clerks and typists, with additional education required for bookkeeping, secretarial, and statistical work. Most upper-level jobs require a college degree.

Compiled with the assistance of: Guitar & Accessories Music Marketing Association, International Association of Electronic Keyboard Manufacturers, Music Industry Conference, National Association of Band Instrument Manufacturers, and Piano Manufacturers Association International.

Music Publishing

Music publishing is a multifaceted field made up of interdependent operations, each involving specific career opportunities. The publishing process begins with the selection of what will be published, whether it is an original musical composition or a new arrangement of an existing piece.

DIRECTORS OF PUBLICATIONS AND EDITORS

In some firms, the selection of pieces to be published is handled by the director of publications, who may also serve as an editor. His or her qualifications almost defy description since the work calls for highly developed musical taste, a strong sense of the market, and an eye on the budget.

Sometimes the director of publications alone accepts, rejects, or commissions a work; sometimes the decision is made by a committee. In other instances, it is made by the head of the music publishing company.

Once the work is accepted for publication, it must be readied for production. An editor reviews the manuscript and makes sure everything is in perfect order, from the proper spelling of the title to the last dynamic mark on the page.

MUSIC PROCESSORS AND PROOFREADERS

When the editor completes his or her work, the manuscript moves on for processing into a form suitable for printing. At one time, most printed music was engraved by hand by etching the music out of a soft metal plate with special tools. Because this method is very time-consuming and requires very skilled workers, it has all but disappeared. Today's music processors transform manuscripts into the familiar style of sheet music by music typewriter, autography, dry transfer of preprinted self-adhering notes and symbols, and increasingly by the use of computer programs that produce high-quality output on sophisticated laser printers.

The processed pages must then be proofread. Sometimes the composer handles this task, but more frequently a professional proofreader makes sure that the music to be printed conforms to the manuscript.

The work is then returned to the processor, who makes the necessary changes, and then it is given a final check by the proofreader.

With the music completed, an artist designs the cover and adds any necessary sketches or photographs. The work is now ready for the final printing.

The background and training of composers, editors, and proofreaders is similar. Although a composer's area of expertise may vary from the proofreader's, both should have as broad a background in all areas of music as possible. An understanding of the composition and arranging processes, of notation of music, of style, and of form related to all types of music is a must.

Although many editors specialize, the broader your base of knowledge the better; the opportunities are much greater if you are well versed in all musical styles. There are, however, situations that call for a specialist with extensive general background coupled with a specific area of expertise (for example, keyboard music of the Baroque era). If you would like to specialize—as an editor, a composer, or an arranger—it would be to your advantage to acquire a solid general background before concentrating on a specific area.

If you are interested in becoming a music processor, an artist, or a printer, an understanding of music is helpful but not absolutely necessary. You will probably be trained on the job or through a special school or instruction program.

After the composition is printed, the next step is to let the public know about it. This is the responsibility of advertising professionals, who need special training in this field. Although it is not essential to have music training, it is necessary to understand the nature of the publications from the vantage point of the musician/consumer.

SPECIALISTS

While these career opportunities are typical throughout the music publishing field, there are a number of other specialized areas, including:
- Standard publishing of master works, special editions, and publication of past and present serious music
- Educational publishing, concentrating on both instructional and performance material for preschool to college levels

- Popular music publishing, revolving around current songs and standards (those that maintain their popularity after their initial success)

Further career opportunities exist in music promotion. Some companies specializing in music for school use lecturers and clinicians to maintain contact with educators who are potential customers.

Companies that publish concert music, ballets, and operas naturally try to encourage the performance of such works. Some large publishers with extensive catalogs in these areas maintain a promotion staff, which may include several full-time employees. These people bring their repertoire to the attention of performing organizations and individual performers through personal contact and written materials such as catalogs, press releases, and newsletters. Smaller companies may assign promotion of such works to a staff member who also has other responsibilities with the company.

In addition to promotion people, publishers with symphonic and operatic catalogs maintain rental libraries to furnish materials for works that are not available for sale. A rental librarian must have a good working knowledge of the requirements of orchestras and other performing groups, as well as the ability to ensure accurate deliveries while working under deadline pressure.

In popular music publishing, a key role is played by the professional manager, whose responsibilities vary from company to company. Generally, however, managers are in charge of acquiring new songs, arranging for their recording, and promoting their performance on radio and television. The professional manager may be assisted by one or more promotion people who work with radio disc jockeys to stimulate airplay.

Although most publishing firms employ outside counsel for complex legal issues, there is a need for a copyright department manager, an in-house employee with a good working knowledge of copyright procedures and their implications for the music publishing business. Much of this knowledge can be obtained through on-the-job training and familiarity with copyright law, the procedures of the United States Copyright Office, protection of rights throughout the world, and other aspects of copyright.

Closely identified with the copyright department manager (and frequently the same person) is the rights and permissions manager. This job involves the licensing of copyrights of the company's music for use in recordings, movies, television films, commercials, and arrangements for publication by others.

The National Association of Recording Arts and Sciences (NARAS) Institute maintains a file on music business courses including those on copyright.

All types of music publishers also require good accounting and book-keeping personnel, and more and more companies are developing data-processing capacity, either in-house or using outside consultants. In addition to the normal accounting and record-keeping requirements of any business (accounts receivable and payable, maintenance of a general ledger, and tax preparation and filing), music publishers are responsible for the payment of royalties to composers and lyricists for sales, rentals, recordings, and all other uses of the works they represent. A musical background is not essential, but a good music publishing accountant or data processor must be comfortable working in a business in which most of the activity is made up of small transactions, all of which must be properly accounted for down to the smallest detail.

Music publishing is, comparatively speaking, a small business. Getting started is largely a matter of determining what career aspect is particularly interesting to you, then knocking on doors.

While there are music publishing companies scattered around the country, the centers for the business have traditionally been the New York metropolitan area, Los Angeles, and Nashville.

Where Do You Fit In?

If you were knowledgeable in all these areas, could you do everything yourself? Well, that's how many people begin in publishing. An individual with a love of music and its presentation in printed form is the potential future publisher.

This type of person is often a specialist in a specific field and has a point of view that he or she wants to convey to others. He or she starts by publishing in this field, performing all the functions previously discussed. As the business expands, others are hired and trained to handle specific functions in the overall production. You can easily see, therefore, that some business background is also very important.

Music publishing offers a unique opportunity to begin your own business. It is one of the few business areas that offers possibilities for the individual working almost completely alone to make things happen for himself or herself and for the people who write and perform music.

Compiled with the assistance of: Music Publishers Association and National Music Publishers Association.

Piano Tuning

A piano tuner/technician tunes, regulates the mechanism to optimum performance, and makes necessary repairs to or replacements of parts on pianos. Most of the work is done in homes, where most pianos are located. Tuner/technicians also work in schools, conservatories, studios, places of worship, concert halls, music stores, and piano rebuilding shops.

Most piano tuner/technicians are independent, relying on their reputations for business and developing a clientele over a period of years. Some, however, work as regular employees of or on contract with schools and music stores.

Besides learning the skills involved in becoming proficient, an independent piano tuner/technician must be personable and capable of personal and business discipline to be successful.

An Acquired Skill

Tuning is an acquired skill not at all related to musical talent or ability to identify pitches. First, your ear must be trained to hear the interference (called beats) caused by two nearly identical frequencies of sound. Also, your mind must be trained to know how to use the speed of beats to establish "equal temperament," usually on a pitch source of standard frequency, such as a tuning fork or an electronic device. Finally, coordination must be developed between the ear and hand manipulating the tuning lever to accomplish minute adjustments of tension in each of a piano's 225-odd strings.

Learning this process and becoming proficient takes time and practice, in many ways like learning to play the instrument. Some electronic frequency comparison devices can aid in learning and practice but are not a substitute for the judgment required of the trained ear in dealing with pianos having varying degrees of inharmonicity.

While the theory of tuning can be learned through a correspondence course or a book, a significant amount of personal instruction interspersed with practice is needed to achieve the right results. Generally, a piano tuner's training must include work on at least one thousand pianos before he or she is able to tune acceptably.

The typical piano tuner of years ago usually had only enough knowledge of piano mechanics to make silent notes play or to patch broken parts. In contrast, today's piano tuner/technician learns to fine-regulate the piano action and keys to factory specifications with a variety of special tools.

Broken or malfunctioning parts on newer pianos can usually be taken care of through replacement and reregulation. If new parts are not readily available for older pianos or if the tuner/technician is working in a remote area, he or she must be able to make or adapt parts that will function correctly. Both the piano student and the accomplished musician have a right to expect that their tuner/technician maintain instruments at optimum levels of mechanical and musical performance. While much can be learned about the piano's mechanism from reading and study, only actual practice under supervision in a residence school, piano shop, or by an independent tuner/technician will assure progress to a satisfactory level of competence.

Specialized Types of Work

Piano tuner/technicians frequently specialize in particular kinds of work. Such specialties might concentrate on keyboard repair, concert and studio piano maintenance (usually possible only in metropolitan areas), or restoration of antique instruments. Not all these specialties require the ability to tune.

Some larger public school systems and many universities and colleges have piano tuner/technicians as full-time staff members and provide shop space, tools, materials, regular hours, and fringe benefits. Because these positions offer almost automatic prestige and security not so easily achieved in independent practice, salaries may be somewhat lower than a well-established person can earn on his or her own. However, because of the requirements of music school faculties, standards for these positions are usually quite high.

In certain areas of the country, music stores employ piano tuner/technicians to do in-home service for which the employee may receive a salary and travel allowance or a commission. In these situations, the store handles the management functions of taking calls, arranging appointments, and collecting fees from customers. Employed tuner/technicians may enjoy fringe benefits they would otherwise have to provide for themselves, plus an assured income, but standards of performance and potential earnings will be dictated by the employer. Working in a store is an excellent way to develop proficiency and gain experience before starting an independent practice.

Personal Freedom and Independence

The personal freedom and independence possible for a well-trained piano tuner/technician, combined with the near-professional relationship with clients and satisfaction of combining intellect and hand to recreate beauty attracts many young men and women to the field. While job success depends on many factors, the fact remains that as long as there are pianos, piano tuner/technicians will be needed.

Earnings for a well-established, full-time piano tuner/technician depend on local rates and time spent traveling to jobs. Of the total earnings, 25 to 30 percent typically would go for operating expenses, overhead, taxes, insurance, and provisions for education and retirement.

Piano tuner/technicians are not regulated or licensed. Voluntary associations are active, however, in establishing standards of professional competence and conduct. The Piano Technicians Guild, for example, offers examinations and certification.

Compiled with the assistance of: National Piano Foundation and Piano Technicians Guild.

CAREERS IN THE RECORDING INDUSTRY

RECORDING ARTISTS AND SONGWRITERS

The lure of music, mystique surrounding recording artists and musicians, and the stereotyped fantasies of show business have encouraged a lot of interest in the recording business as a career. But, despite the high sales and visibility of the recording industry, job opportunities are not abundant or easy to come by.

Some men and women realize their dreams, but most do not. There is no formula for breaking into the business or any one technique that will allow you to zoom ahead of the competition.

While there are several recording centers in this country (Los Angeles, New York, Chicago, Nashville, San Francisco, Memphis, Atlanta), there are recording studios throughout the United States. Often your chances of getting that first break are better in a less competitive community.

The recording industry is fragmented, consisting of some large organizations and hundreds of small ones. If you want to get into the business of producing and selling records, talk to other people already in the recording industry, record stores, record companies, recording studios—anywhere a staff member can help you separate the facts from the myths.

Basic Skills, Personal Attributes

Regardless of which recording industry specialty you want to pursue, there are some basic skills and personal attributes you should have:

- working knowledge of music, including theory, arranging, and composition
- flexibility in adapting your talents to all kinds of music
- reliability in meeting deadlines and commitments

All recordings of popular music start with a song, either written for a specific artist or a standard that has been rearranged. Some songwriters work through a publisher; others publish their own works. Songs can be brought to the attention of performers, recording companies, or artist and repertoire (A&R) people by publishing companies or by songwriters themselves.

Following are descriptions of jobs directly related to the production and distribution of a record. For all of these jobs, you should work at becoming a master of your craft and get to know people already in the field. Once you have experience, landing a job at a major record company or a big-city recording center becomes less difficult.

RECORD PRODUCER AND A&R PERSON

These professionals may be employed by a record company, by the artist, or work independently. They are the liaisons between publishers, artists, and record companies, matching songs with musicians to produce a commercially successful sound. Duties include finding new artists, locating fresh material for established singers and groups, hiring arrangers and copyists, preparing the recording session budget, and getting authorization to spend money or raise funds from outside sources. The producer then works with an engineer to create the vocal and instrumental combination that will sell records.

Major recording companies hire A&R specialists who have proven themselves as successful producers and have demonstrated a talent for creating best-sellers. Job advancement in this area depends on the ability to produce results at the point of sale.

To get production experience you may want to consider working with a promising band that would like to cut a record. Sometimes a group's personal manager will raise money for a recording session and "A&R" it. Occasionally, an arranger or conductor will insist on handling production duties to ensure that the music is recorded as written. Songwriters and publishers also have an opportunity to produce when they record demonstration records or tapes.

STUDIO ARRANGER

Arrangers can be free-lance or affiliated with a particular studio. They score songs for the group and the instruments used in the recording session. The arranger may be a songwriter scoring his or her own works, be a member of a performing group, or work full-time at arranging. Arrangers' fees are set by union contracts based on number of score pages: the more scores an arranger prepares, the higher the fee. Many arrangers work nights; daytime hours are spent answering inquiries and sometimes conducting.

If you want to become an arranger, it is important to read music quickly and write neatly. While you do not have to play any instruments well, it is very important that you have a working knowledge of each instrument for which you might be scoring, including their timbres, temperaments, and ranges. You will also need a strong sense of what is currently popular and an instinct for future trends.

COPYIST

The music copyist transcribes the arranger's score for each musician or group of instruments and may be hired directly by a record company, master producer, arranger, or music department of a film or television production company.

Working hours are very irregular. Fees are set by union contract and vary depending on amount of music, type of instrument, and type of paper used.

To become a copyist, you must read music and write legibly, rapidly, and accurately; knowledge of musical theory and harmony is also helpful. As a copyist, you will become acquainted with a great deal of music written for the commercial market and will have the chance to meet many influential people in the recording business. Many copyists often move on to careers as arrangers.

MUSIC CONTRACTOR

The music contractor steps in after the A&R person has decided the instrumental and vocal complement for a recording session. The union contractor ensures that all musicians to be called are members of the American Federation of Musicians (AFofM) and that vocalists are members of the American Federation of Television and Radio Artists (AFTRA).

At the session, the contractor is the expert on union rules, settles any problems, makes sure each person receives income tax deduction forms, and files a report with the AFofM and AFTRA about the hours worked and personnel involved. To qualify as a union contractor you must be a musician, be a union member, and be familiar with contract rules and regulations, performance capabilities and specialties of various musicians in your area, and music preferences of different A&R people.

Hours are very irregular since the union contractor sets the session during business hours and sits in when recordings are made. Some contractors also may participate in sessions as musicians. Therefore, musicians may want to look for producers who are willing to appoint them union contractor.

MUSICIAN LEADER

These professionals organize singers, instrumentalists, and background vocalists into one performing group. Frequently, the leader also may write arrangements and conduct. Leaders make sure musicians perform well and within time allocated for the session. They are paid double the scale of a musician. Several leaders have risen from the ranks of studio musicians while others are arranger/conductors. Occasionally, the musician leader may also act as the session's union contractor.

RECORDING MUSICIANS OR SIDEMEN

Recording musicians play in most recording sessions unless a symphony orchestra or cast and orchestra of a Broadway play is featured. Without exception, recording musicians are highly skilled pros who sight-read music and normally give the A&R person, the arranger, the songwriter, or the conductor the right sounds on the first try. Delays at recording sessions are very expensive and avoided as much as possible. Sometimes sidemen will suggest routine or inventive changes, but arguments about arrangements are not tolerated. The recording musician must be able to cooperate fully, regardless of personal musical style or taste.

Preparing for a career as a studio musician means developing good performance skills so you can play almost any kind of music after reading the score. To get experience, participate in school music ensembles, join friends in groups, play in family get-togethers, or study music in college.

To get into this recording area, start visiting anyone who might be hiring musicians: recording studios, record companies, publishers, songwriters. Leave a business card on the chance there might be a job available in the future. Sometimes, arrangers and contractors may find their first-choice musicians are unavailable and call on friends or business associates as substitute sidemen.

RECORDING ENGINEERS OR MIXERS

The engineer sets up microphones and operates equipment necessary to record the session according to the instructions of the A&R person. The producer may give presession instructions to the engineer, including a studio floor plan showing instrumental groupings, microphone placement, and the acoustical baffles to be used.

The engineer is concerned with five areas: musical range, rhythm, variety, dynamics, and spectral control. The engineer must be able to compensate for studio limitations, the recording medium, and reproduction equipment.

Since engineering is one of the most popular career areas in recording, studios are extremely selective in hiring. To prepare yourself, enroll in a college that offers specific courses in sound engineering, learn to operate all technical machines, read the trade magazines, and visit recording studios. Try to get a studio job to learn more about the capabilities of the equipment.

MERCHANDISERS, MANAGERS, AND OTHERS

In addition to creating and producing records, the recording industry offers many job opportunities on the business side. Often, these jobs give valuable insights into what makes a record a success.

The very nature of recordings also fragments many of the functions into product types. There are often different companies, departments, or labels within a company, which produce classical, rock, country-western, soul, ethnic, or spoken-word records.

The recording industry is oriented to smallness. In almost every job category mentioned here there are individuals and small independent enterprises that go it alone. Often, these represent the best opportunities for a newcomer to break into the field and eventually become an entrepreneur.

- Selling the completed record directly to retailers and wholesalers in a given geographic area is a great way to learn the business. You appraise product requirements, take orders, introduce new records, evaluate stock, merchandise the product, and arrange for advertising and merchandising programs. Salespeople often start as part of the junior sales staff or as order or inventory clerks. Sales personnel may work directly for record companies, independent distributors, or rack jobbers (who keep stores, especially mass merchandizers, supplied with the latest releases).
- Merchandising is a sales-support function within a record company that includes developing communication programs to help sell the product and having responsibility for advertising, display, customer communications, sales staff communication, and sales literature.
- Promotion in the recording industry usually is geared toward radio and television. Duties are devoted to maximizing the recording's airplay through personal contact with management and broadcast personnel.
- Graphics are important to the recording business in packaging, display work, and merchandising units. An entire graphics industry is peripheral to the recording business, and many opportunities are available in this related field.
- Manufacturing jobs vary from unskilled labor to skilled production work and sophisticated control and management responsibilities. Not all record companies manufacture their own records and tapes, but thousands of jobs are open to meet the production requirements of the industry.
- General management involves various levels of administrative and executive jobs filled by generalists and specialists in the industry. Most of these people move up the ranks by demonstrating unusual skills.

DISC JOCKEYS

The disc jockey (DJ) combines the skills of a lively commentator with a knowledge of current musical trends and technical ability to operate equipment in the broadcasting studio.

Airplay by a DJ can have an important and far-reaching effect on record sales. The DJ schedules music, prepares ad lib introductions for commercials, conducts quizzes and contests, and sometimes produces spot announcements for the radio station. At larger stations, the DJ may work with the music director and program manager to select music that fits the station's format: middle-of-the-road, young adult and contemporary, "golden oldies," or preteen rock. The DJ may also have a show that appeals to a specific segment of the station's general audience.

DJs may have an engineer to help them during regular office hours but may be required to do their own technical work in the early morning or late evening. Since DJs try to build a personal following to maintain high audience ratings for the station, they frequently make free or paid appearances at sponsors' places of business, dances, clubs, and other promotional events where they can meet the public and their fans.

If you want to become a disc jockey, it is important to combine your music studies with courses in English and public speaking. Take radio courses in high school if they are available and, of course, study radio in college. Visit local radio stations to see DJs at work. Learn all you can about currently popular artists and songs by listening to records and radio. Study the styles of different DJs so you can develop one that fits your personality.

Practice by working at your school's radio station. Programming records for school social events, such as dances, is good experience for radio programming. Tape your appearances to play back later so you can analyze your performance.

After you have graduated and are ready for a job, first try the smaller stations, where you may have more leeway in music scheduling and programming.

MUSIC INDUSTRY ATTORNEYS

The music industry attorney is a specialist in copyright structure, restrictions on publications, mechanical reproductions, and performance rights licensing. This type of attorney must understand union agreements, terms and conditions of publisher contracts, problems of independent master producers, record and tape distribution and methods of accounting, record and tape retailing, promotional practices, artist and manager agreements, and the problems and potential of the videocassette. In addition, music industry attorneys handle all nonmusic business and personal legal matters of their clients. Naturally you must become a lawyer first, but if you want to specialize in music-related law, it helps to learn the business early.

There is no right way to get started in any of these jobs. You will have to knock on doors, be persistent, and be creative. Be direct and simple in your résumé, but do not overlook creative ways to enter a creative business.

Compiled with the assistance of: Recording Industry Association of America.

CAREERS IN
ALLIED FIELDS

Music Therapy

Using music to influence changes in behavior and to assist with a variety of functions is known as music therapy. Although it is often thought of as a recent addition to the health care field, music therapy's roots can be traced back to the beginning of recorded civilization. Music and healing have been entwined throughout most of human existence, and the functional role of music in most societies has been equal to, if not paramount to, its artistic role.

Music therapy uses music and music activities directed by a trained music therapist to maintain, restore, and improve emotional, cognitive, and physical health. The overall treatment strategy is to enable the individual to function more successfully within his or her environment. Music therapists work in psychiatric facilities, mental retardation centers, rehabilitation centers, schools, community mental health centers, day care centers, nursing homes, special education schools, hospices, prisons, and many other health care facilities.

The basic music therapy process is applicable to many different treatment settings. The materials and techniques used are often transferable from one type of disability to another. Because music therapy is used in a variety of settings, it is a logical career choice for anyone interested in combining music with personal service.

A Recognized Treatment

Whether your interest lies with children, the elderly, or persons with particular learning or physical disabilities or emotional illnesses, music therapy is a recognized treatment used by many health service institutions.

If you want to become a music therapist, you should take every opportunity in high school to excel on your chosen musical instrument, as well as get some experience conducting instrumental and vocal groups. You should also be able to play piano, and by all means try to find a teacher who is knowledgeable in this specialized teaching technique. Proficiency on a number of instruments is required.

Getting Experience

To get experience, you can volunteer at one of many local health care facilities. Some students find summer jobs working with children or adults with disabilities in places such as camps or day treatment facilities.

College preparation for music therapy mainly focuses on music, psychology, and the social sciences. You not only must demonstrate proficiency on your major instrument, but also must develop skill on a variety of instruments such as guitar, piano, recorder, and others associated with folk music. While in college, you will get experience in clinical practices by observing and conducting activities at treatment facilities.

Following college course work, you will complete a six-month clinical training internship at one of more than 150 approved treatment institutions around the country. Successful completion of a music therapy degree and clinical training internship qualifies you to apply for the status of Registered Music Therapist with the National Association for Music Therapy (NAMT) as well as be eligible for certification in music therapy.

A standard baccalaureate music therapy curriculum, totaling 133 semester hours, has been developed by NAMT and is offered by more than sixty-five universities. Course work is required in the following areas: Music Therapy (minimum of 20 semester hours); Psychology, Sociology, Health Sciences (minimum of 20 semester hours); Music (60 semester hours); General Education (27 semester hours); General Electives (6 semester hours).

Professional music therapy courses in the theory and practice of music therapy are taught by competent instructors who have an extensive background in music therapy. A master's degree is offered at a number of universities around the country. The minimum requirement for teaching music therapy at the college level includes a master's degree plus two years of clinical experience as a therapist.

A Growing Field

This field is not only growing but also changing. Several decades ago, few institutions, except psychiatric hospitals, included music therapy in their treatment programs. Gradually, as institutions of all types began examining the traditional forms of treatment offered, more experimentation with alternative methods of treatment was undertaken. Music therapy, one of those alternatives, is now found in a wide variety and an increasing number of institutions.

Working conditions vary considerably depending on the nature of the facility, the number of patients involved, and the treatment philosophy. While music therapists work with a basic plan of therapy, flexibility is required. A therapist normally works in one institution with groups of patients, although it may be necessary to work with individuals on a one-to-one basis. Therapy schedules may range from several times a week with small groups to less frequent sessions with larger groups. Salaries, too, vary with the size of the facility, its location, and its budget.

Compiled with the assistance of: National Association for Music Therapy.

Music Libraries

As a music librarian, you are first a musician in the broadest sense of the word, because music of any style, medium, or era may find a place in a library. And you are also a librarian. Aptitude and training in both fields are necessary.

Music librarians work in several kinds of libraries. Large music research libraries, such as those at the Library of Congress and the New York Public Library, employ a number of music librarians with comparatively specialized functions. These institutions serve a large public and answer a wide variety of questions, from complex research problems for musicological scholars to the location of obscure or out-of-print music for nationally known concert artists or the person on the street. Librarians in these institutions acquire and integrate every kind of music and everything written about music into their enormous collections.

University and Public Library Positions

Most universities, conservatories, and many colleges have separate music libraries headed by professional music librarians. Such libraries usually offer research and reference facilities and circulating collections, including scores and performing parts.

As a university music librarian, you will work with the faculty to develop a library that meets the needs of students and provides more literature and information for the advanced or curious student. You also will cooperate with performing ensembles in the school, often helping orchestras, opera workshop presenters, or chamber ensembles find the music they require.

Large public libraries in major cities frequently have either a separate music, a combination music and art, or a performing arts (including dance and drama) section. Such libraries usually have large circulating collections of recordings in addition to scores and music books. Music librarians here need a wide knowledge of popular and serious music and must be particularly aware of current musical trends.

Even smaller public libraries that cannot employ a music librarian exclusively often have collections of circulating records requiring the supervision of someone with musical knowledge. Also, public libraries often sponsor music recitals or festivals or produce programs for local radio or television.

Certain special libraries also serve the music field. Radio and television stations may have their own libraries. Large music publishers and organizations, such as the American Society of Composers, Authors and Publishers (ASCAP), sometimes hire music librarians to organize and deal with their holdings. Music retailers, too, often find library training valuable in their profession.

Orchestra librarians, whose main function is to acquire instrumental works for an orchestra and prepare them for performance, occupy a somewhat special category in that they are not usually professional librarians. For this job, the ability to read and write music fluently and legibly is more important than the reference and cataloging skills used by other music librarians.

A Variety of Duties

Since music libraries are comparatively small and specialized to begin with, as a music librarian you often have to assume several different functions: administrator; reference specialist; and liaison with the public, faculty, and library staff.

Only the music cataloger is likely to work within a rather restricted sphere. The cataloger works comparatively alone, preparing catalog entries and subject headings and classifying new material according to the system used in a particular library. Cataloging can be an intellectually challenging task if there is a variety of material to be considered.

Outside of large research libraries, most institutions do not employ more than two or three music librarians, with a cataloger and perhaps a recording specialist to assist the head music librarian. Salaries are not high.

The field is not large and there is a consequent lack of mobility in the higher positions. Attractive openings are not always easy to find, especially if geographical considerations are important. Most jobs are located in cities or in college and university communities. Some of these, New York for example, are more popular than others. Even excellent qualifications do not always guarantee the prospective music librarian the position that he or she might prefer.

On the positive side, music librarianship can be consistently interesting to the intellectually curious person. Routine tasks are constantly varied by changing needs of the library and its patrons. Music librarians come in contact with many areas and aspects of music; a few minutes of a librarian's day may include helping a young flute student, a local opera director, a Japanese koto player, and a teenage fan of country fiddling. You are in a position to serve student and teacher, professional and amateur, composer and critic. Like many people in the music field, music librarians frequently participate in other musical activities in their spare time. Many music librarians are also performers, composers, critics, or musicologists.

Recommended Preparation

As librarianship is essentially an academic pursuit, intellectual curiosity and competence are requisites for success. People in the technical services connected with libraries, such as cataloging, often work behind the scenes. Most music librarians, however, have to work with people, so a confident, outgoing personality is definitely an asset. Perhaps the most important sign that you would be happy as a librarian is a deep love of books.

Training for music librarianship should include as broad an education as possible in all aspects of music and liberal arts, supplemented by graduate training in librarianship. Most successful music librarians did not choose this field early in their schooling because, although it is rather small, the background required is immense, and only a student of varied interests is likely to accumulate the kind of knowledge a good music librarian needs. In many positions, a second master's degree (in addition to the library science master's or a Ph.D. in musicology) is required. Graduate study, including a thorough course in music bibliography, is desirable. Experience as a performing musician also is valuable; it gives the librarian practical experience in the requirements of many library users and acquaints him or her more intimately with a specific musical repertoire.

Foreign Language Skills

Since information about music and musical editions is likely to be published in any country and in any language, music librarians should have working knowledge of German and at least one Romance language to do the most basic cataloging or bibliographic research. In addition to languages and history of literature of music, the undergraduate should study a wide variety of liberal arts, history, literature, art, and philosophy, because music librarians need to be able to draw on information and resources from other disciplines as well as their own specialties.

Because of the knowledge to be accumulated, formal training in librarianship usually comes rather late in the educational process. Most accredited schools of library science offer graduate programs of at least thirty-six credits, culminating in the Master of Library Science degree, which is required for most professional jobs. These programs offer training in theory and practice of librarianship, bibliography, reference, acquisition, cataloging, and administration. Some schools offer special courses in music librarianship or joint programs in music and librarianship. While these can be very valuable, you should know that there is no shortcut to acquiring the knowledge a music librarian needs to have.

If you think this might be an interesting, satisfying career, the best way to find out is to work part-time in a library. Libraries usually have places for college or high school students to help shelve books and perform minor clerical tasks. Knowledge of typing can help you advance at the clerical level, but simply being in and part of the library will acquaint you with many of its operations. Working hours are usually flexible and conditions are pleasant if you like books; many students use the opportunity to earn extra money even if they have no plans to stay in library work. Practical experience working in a library also can be invaluable when and if you decide to go to library school.

Compiled with the assistance of: Music Library Association.

Music Criticism

A music critic's job is not easy to define, particularly since there are not yet universally accepted standards for this profession. As a critic, it will not be your purpose simply to give a "report card" to performing musicians but to make a meaningful contribution to the art that nurtures them; at the same time, you will be helping to expand the active audience by writing about music in a way that portrays it as a vital and stimulating experience.

Specific duties of a music critic vary from one publication to another, depending on size of staff and community. A large metropolitan newspaper may have a staff of music specialists assigned to opera, early music, experimental music, and so on, and critics who review recordings but not live events. At smaller newspapers, a single critic may cover not only all musical events but drama, dance, films, and other arts as well. In addition to actual reviewing, most critics (as differentiated from reviewers) are expected to editorialize occasionally about events of unusual importance, the state of the art, or problems within the music community.

Speak the Language

One of America's most respected senior critics suggested that criticism should begin with a basic understanding between the critic and the person subject to his or her criticism; they should speak the same language. He also suggested that all critics need musical training.

The fundamental problem, as this critic pointed out, is that the selection of critics is often slanted toward writers who know more or less about music rather than toward musicians who know more or less about writing. Most respected critics agree that they need to be knowledgeable musicians capable of expressing themselves, rather than merely skilled wordsmiths with a smattering of musical knowledge.

The Music Critics Association, the professional organization of American and Canadian critics, considers the education of critics and establishment of recognized standards to be among its prime objectives; the association has been sponsoring summer institutes and workshops for critics in cooperation with music festivals and universities for several years and is in contact with a number of colleges and universities regarding possibilities of creating a degree program in criticism.

What You Should Know

Boris Nelson, a former president of the Music Critics Association, offers this list of requirements for the aspiring critic:

- a thorough musical background, historical and practical, that is, theoretical and basic knowledge of instrumentation with actual ability to play an instrument
- a good ear; good genetically, but also trained and tuned
- the ability to write clearly and to the point for the readership of a specific publication
- constant listening and writing, augmented by general reading in the arts, history, and the world at large
- the ability to identify personal preferences and dislikes and to separate them from judgment-making in the interest of objectivity
- involvement; a love for things musical, a high degree of enthusiasm and even idealism that communicates itself to the reader
- the willingness to stand up for a justifiable opinion, supported by knowledge, fairness, and experience

In short, you need passion for music, the drive to communicate it and the skill to make yourself understood. At the same time, you need the self-discipline to be dispassionate in your judgments. Ideally, the music critic should write with such conviction and enthusiasm that the reader, who may never have been particularly moved by music, thinks "What have I been missing?" He or she should never write down to that group of readers, nor try to impress more musically sophisticated readers with technical displays that could be of interest only to fellow critics and scholars.

Getting Started

This field is not expanding. Several major journals have cut back on general coverage of the arts; some have ceased publication. One possible entrée into this field is through a related activity, such as broadcasting, program annotation, or public relations work for musical organizations.

A more direct way is to apply for a position as assistant or junior critic at a newspaper or magazine with a staff large enough to include such positions or to apply for "stringer" status. Stringers are not staff members, but are called in on an as-needed basis to review a particular event. Junior critics, assistants, and stringers are frequently the first to get the nod when a bigger job opens up, either at their own publication or another.

Once you are in on the ground floor of a large-scale operation, you will probably find yourself doing chores for senior colleagues; writing the daily or weekly calendar of musical events, researching details to accompany the senior critic's major review, keeping the schedule of department assignments, finding pictures to use with the reviews. These duties acquaint the junior critic with the importance of these details, which the critic on a smaller paper, or in a one-person department, must look after personally.

Interviews are also part of the critic's job, which means you must be familiar with the work and outlook of significant music personalities. The ability to be entertaining in such writing, as well as in reviews themselves, is a substantial asset, as long as it is kept in reasonable proportion to the main objective.

Informing and Stimulating Readers

Even the most successful critics cannot expect financial rewards like those realized by people making similar commitments in industry or other professions. They can, however, enjoy a feeling of considerable fulfillment; not in terms of being recognized in a restaurant or having reviews quoted, but in helping inform and stimulate the laypersons and musicians among their readers.

A critic's ideas can help expand the repertoire of the performer, concertgoer, and record collector. The research a critic does, or ought to do, in preparing to write about a major performance or recording may add substantially to the general background and understanding of a given work, composer, or entire period in music history.

Traveling to report on premieres and festivals in other cities and countries can be one benefit of the work. Few publications, however, have budgets to support such assignments; more often, it may be the industrious freelancer with arrangements to supply several different publications with reports on the same event who does the traveling.

In addition to the periodic workshops, seminars, and institutes offered by the Music Critics Association, master's degree programs in music criticism are offered at both the Peabody Conservatory of the Johns Hopkins University in Baltimore and at McMaster University in Hamilton, Ontario.

Compiled with the assistance of: Music Critics Association.

Music Communications

If you like music and also think you have writing skills, you may want to combine them in one of many jobs within the communications field. Consider the many places you read about music: on recordings, in symphony programs, in advertisements for musical instruments, in newspaper and magazine articles, and in the booklets that come with a new instrument. The fields of publicity, public relations, advertising, reporting, and writing educational materials are just a few of the related communications specialties in which you can use your musical knowledge.

PUBLICITY

Working with publicity is the business of making certain your client is well represented in the media. If you read a newspaper or magazine story about a musical group, for example, chances are a publicist was involved in making that story a reality. Publicists generally are responsible for preparing copy about their clients, making contact with the media, and suggesting ideas for news and feature stories that deal favorably with the product, person, or group they represent. Most well-known musicians employ publicists, as do most recording companies, musical groups, and organizations. Not everyone makes a good publicist. You need writing ability, a sense of creativity about what makes news, and personal integrity.

PUBLIC RELATIONS

Professionals in this field need sharp communications skills requiring in-depth knowledge of the subject, as well as communication techniques and good business practice. Public relations specialists use publicity as one of their tools, but they usually are involved in a variety of activities to develop a favorable image for their client. Musical instrument manufacturers, music associations, and educator groups are far more likely to employ public relations experts than people whose skill is limited to publicity.

Public relations specialists should be able to write clearly and concisely for all types of media. Most important, they must understand the far-reaching consequences of communications challenges and be able to plan effectively to deal with them.

If you are interested in publicity or public relations, the best training is writing. You may want to enroll in a journalism school or pursue a public relations curriculum that is now offered by many college and universities. However, if you can major in business with a minor in journalism, you will probably be best prepared for a public relations career.

ADVERTISING

Advertising is selling a company, its products, or a musical organization through paid messages in newspapers and magazines or on radio or television. Advertising work is handled both by independent agencies serving all facets of the music business and by in-house staffs (advertising and promotion departments maintained within a company to prepare print ads and commercials). Often, companies employ a combination of the two.

If you want a career in music advertising, the field is somewhat limited; you would be better advised to plan a broad enough education to handle any advertising job rather than focus entirely on music. A college degree in marketing and advertising is highly recommended.

REPORTING

Reporting for newspapers, magazines, radio, or television may involve covering community music events as news, writing about the music industry, interviewing musicians, or covering local school music programs. Unless you work for a music trade publication that covers the music business exclusively, reporting for other media will mean covering events that go far beyond music.

You can get experience by working on your high school or college newspaper, or at a radio or television station. Getting writing experience is the best way to develop the proficiency you will need to handle a professional job. A journalism major is recommended.

WRITING EDUCATIONAL MATERIALS

Educational materials constitute a very important part of the communications effort by publishing firms and musical instrument manufacturers.

Both businesses need skilled writers who know a great deal about music. A writer developing educational materials might prepare a brochure about flute playing techniques, edit an entire magazine that goes to music educators, or even write a book.

If you are interested in music education and writing, this area offers a very rewarding career. Knowledge of music is vital, but the ability to express your thoughts clearly and succinctly should also be developed though writing courses and as many writing assignments as you can handle. For any or all of these various career opportunities, start developing your writing skills now. Consider handling promotion or publicity for your school music group, becoming a music reporter for the school newspaper, offering your services to the community newspaper, or volunteering as publicity agent for a local band or orchestra.

Getting Practical Experience

The more practical experience you bring to your first job interview, the more likely you are to land it. Competition is strong and openings for the spot you want are limited. You may have to work your way up to the assignments you desire.

Job opportunities as publicists are available in most cities around the country, but unless you find work in New York, Los Angeles, or Chicago, you may not be paid well enough to make this a full-time job. Many public relations firms in these three cities have music-related accounts, but do not forget that every symphony orchestra also needs publicity and public relations help no matter where it is located. Public relations firms prefer writers with experience at newspapers, or magazines, or in the electronic media.

The major music trade publications are also located in Chicago, New York, and Los Angeles, but newspapers all around the country have general assignment reporters who may have music included in their beats.

Advertising agencies draw their staffs from writers who have gained experience in retail advertising or by working directly for individual companies or at smaller agencies.

Some companies do hire beginners with exceptional talent or who have gone through an internship connected with their college degree. Large newspapers hire students out of school, but if you want to get a sure start it is wise to work first on a small newspaper or magazine.

Research the firms for which you would like to work. Read music trade magazines. Get to know the advertising and public relations agencies that represent your chosen field, and watch what they do. Get to know people in the communications field. Join student chapters of professional associations and attend meetings. You will be able to find out more about the jobs available in the community, know where the openings are, and have access to job opportunities not generally known about. If the job you want is not immediately available, take one that will help you reach your ultimate goal. Always take advantage of opportunities to work with musical organizations on a volunteer basis and build up your writing portfolio of music-related articles, ads, or publicity.

Your perseverance, enthusiasm, and natural talents will help you reach your career goal; communicating the enjoyment of music to others.

Compiled with the assistance of: American Music Conference.

Music for Worship

Careers in music for worship can be as numerous and varied as places of worship themselves. However, these career opportunities have in common the chance to lead others in music-making and help the church enrich people's lives through music. Just as denominations differ, even churches and synagogues within a given denomination or tradition can be very different. Size, locale, resources, traditions, even competition, can make job opportunities in one parish as different as day and night from those in another.

Types of Opportunities

There may be job opportunities for a full-time music director who has overall responsibility for all music in a given church or synagogue; such a job may call for an assistant to serve as organist. In other institutions, large and small, the organist and choirmaster may be one person who has an assistant depending on size and budget of the parish. In some churches, responsibility for music may be given to people who perform dual functions. Director of music duties might be combined with youth work, for example, or education, business management, or direction of creative arts where music is only one aspect of the job.

Salaries are usually higher for combination jobs but may require a broad background to handle responsibilities well. The director of music and youth work, for example, must have the music background described above and an understanding of young people. Such a dual job may require not only a thorough grasp of vocal and instrumental music, but also an understanding of dramatics and dancing. The director of music and education must, of course, have a thorough grounding in the basics of religious education and know how to plan and direct programs for both young and old. The musician who doubles as music director and business manager will also need to learn the basics of management.

The director of creative arts combines music with a program that involves all arts, including dance, drama, and graphic arts. Such jobs are rare and involve a broad grasp of many disciplines.

Qualifications

In the beginning you will need talent, technique, and the drive and self-discipline to put that ability to work. The church musician needs the capacity to handle the human relations.

A choir director in a religious institution needs a thorough understanding and knowledge of music fundamentals, harmony, theory, counterpoint, the human voice, choral and instrumental conducting, a basic keyboard facility, old and new choral and organ repertoire, liturgies, hymnody, and history. Regardless of the denomination or tradition you plan to serve, it will be important to understand all traditions from Gregorian chant to current rock music.

An organist should have an understanding of the instrument and its literature, as well as technique and repertoire. Recital or solo playing, leading a congregation in singing, and accompanying choirs and soloists all require different skills. It is possible for a gifted recitalist to be a poor service player and vice versa. You need a feel for worship to lift it above the limitations of mere language and tie together different parts of a service.

The ability to improvise can be an important asset. This ability can be developed to a point in almost any organist, although some will have greater skills than others. Outside of progressive jazz, there is probably no area where improvisation can be used to such advantage.

Educational Requirements

If you are considering the field of music for worship, involve yourself in as many musical activities as possible in high school and at your church or synagogue. You will want to take private vocal and instrumental lessons, sing in a school choral group, and maybe take part in the choir at your family's place of worship. You should look for chances to conduct others and play in an instrumental ensemble. Try to develop your sense of rhythm and pitch and train your ears to hear musical sounds and detect subtle differences in the music to which you listen.

After high school, you may want to choose a college, university, or music school specializing in music for worship and further your preparation with music and general courses related to the demands of a career in this field. (Degrees are necessary if you are looking for a job at a major church or synagogue.) It is important also to get practical experience in leading or accompanying music in actual services. Many colleges not only offer, but require, such field experience as part of their curriculum. Such experience sometimes enables a student to earn a small salary while helping a place of worship.

Your own education in music for worship and related subjects should continue even after your formal schooling is complete. Learn what is currently happening, not only in your own denomination or tradition but in others, so you can make a greater, more knowledgeable contribution to your own religious group.

Across the country are countless workshops, seminars, and courses to help in your continuing education. In the late fall, church music journals begin listing summer courses. Overseas, Britain's Royal School of Church Music offers a summer course specifically designed for Americans, which helps students learn firsthand from professional church musicians (cathedral organists and others) who must supply music for services seven days a week.

Church choral programs can vary from a huge multiple-choir setup involving 1,200 volunteer singers in one church to the sophisticated, paid men-and-boy choir programs you may find in a metropolitan church.

More and more, musicians seem to be veering away from an exclusive reliance on the four-part, choral-and-organ sound traditionally associated with church music. Many new anthems and hymns call for unusual accompaniments or no accompaniment at all. There is more use of unison singing, choir and congregational refrain songs, and auxiliary instruments, which provide variety and varied musical textures. Many institutions of worship find extra, purely musical programs can be a rewarding and enjoyable way for the church to make contact with people in the community. In addition to regular services and extra musical programs for the community, a church organist will have responsibility for other services, weddings, and funerals: these events can help supplement his or her income.

Budgets and job openings for full-time musicians at places of worship are limited. But those who pursue full-time or even part-time careers in this field seem to find such work challenging and satisfying.

If you are interested in a religious music career, talk to organists, choir directors, and clergy in your community. Their experience and advice can be invaluable in helping you chart your next steps.

Compiled with the assistance of: American Guild of Organists, Church Music Association of America, Royal School of Church Music, and Sacred Music Magazine.

DIRECTORY OF
MUSIC-RELATED
INFORMATION SOURCES

Air Force Bands, Director of Personnel, Air Force Band and Music Branch (SAF/PAGB), Department of the Air Force, Washington, DC 20330-1000: 202-695-0019.

American Bandmasters Association, 110 Wyanoke Drive, San Antonio, TX 78209, c/o Dr. Jon R. Piersol, Associate Dean, School of Music, Florida State University, Tallahassee, FL 32306: 904-644-5848.

American Choral Directors Association, PO Box 6310, Lawton, OK 73506: 405-355-8161.

American Choral Foundation, c/o Chorus America, 2111 Sansom Street, Philadelphia, PA 19103: 215-563-2430.

American Federation of Musicians of the United States and Canada, AFL-CIO, 1501 Broadway, Suite 600, New York, NY 10036: 212-869-1330.

American Federation of Television and Radio Artists (AFTRA), 260 Madison Avenue, New York, NY 10016: 212-532-0800.

American Guild of Organists, 475 Riverside Drive, Suite 1260, New York, NY 10115: 212-870-2310.

American Music Conference, 303 East Wacker Drive, Suite 1214, Chicago, IL 60601: 312-856-8820.

American Orff-Schulwerk Association, PO Box 391089, Cleveland, OH 44139-1089: 216-543-5366.

American School Band Directors Association, PO Box 146, Otsego, MI 49078: 616-694-2092.

American Society of Composers, Authors and Publishers (ASCAP), One Lincoln Plaza, New York, NY 10023: 212-595-3050.

American Society of Music Copyists, 1697 Broadway, Room 805, New York, NY 10019: 212-586-2140.

American String Teachers Association, University of Georgia Station, Box 2066, Athens, GA 30612: 404-542-2741.

American Symphony Orchestra League, 777 14th Street NW, Suite 500, Washington, DC 20005: 202-628-0099.

Aspen Music School, 250 W. 54th Street, 10th Floor, East, New York, NY 10019: 212-581-2196.

Association of Performing Arts Presenters, 1112 16th Street NW, Suite 620, Washington, DC 20036: 202-833-2787.

Association for Technology in Music Instruction, c/o Ann Blombach, 101 Hughes Hall, 1899 College Road, Ohio State University, Columbus, OH 43210: 614-292-2138.

Audio Engineering Society, 60 East 42nd Street, Room 2520, New York, NY 10165: 212-661-8528.

Broadcast Music, Inc. (BMI), 320 W. 57th Street, New York, NY 10019: 212-586-2000.

Church Music Association of America, c/o Msgr. Richard J. Schuler, 548 Lafond Avenue, St. Paul, MN 55103: 612-293-1710.

College Band Directors National Association, c/o Richard L. Floyd, Box 8028, University of Texas, Austin, TX 78713: 512-471-5883.

The College Music Society, PO Box 18000, Boulder, CO 80308: 303-449-1611.

Conductor's Guild, Inc., PO Box 3361, West Chester, PA 19381: 215-463-4904.

Electronic Music Consortium, c/o Thomas Wells, School of Music, Ohio State University, Columbus, OH 43210: 614-292-6571.

Guitar & Accessories Music Marketing Association, 136 W. 21st Street, New York, NY 10011: 212-924-9175.

Interlochen Center for the Arts, PO Box 199, Interlochen, MI 49643-0199: 616-276-9221.

International Association of Electronic Keyboard Manufacturers, c/o Glenn DePue, Yamaha Corporation of America, Keyboard, PO Box 6600, Buena Park, CA 90620: 714-522-9300.

International Association of Piano Builders and Technicians, c/o Piano Technicians Guild, 4510 Belleview, Suite 100, Kansas City, MO 64111: 816-753-7747.

International MIDI Association, 5316 West 57th Street, Los Angeles, CA 90056: 213-649-6434.

Music Critics Association, 7 Pine Court, Westfield, NJ 07090: 201-233-8468.

Music Distributors Association, 136 W. 21st Street, New York, NY 10011: 212-924-9175.

Music Educators National Conference, 1902 Association Drive, Reston, VA 22091-1597: 703-860-4000.

Music Industry Conference, 1902 Association Drive, Reston, VA 22091-1597: 703-860-4000.

Music Library Association, PO Box 487, Canton, MA 02021: 617-828-8540.

Music Publishers Association, 130 West 57th Street, New York, NY 10019, 212-582-1122.

Music Teachers National Association, 617 Vine Street #1432, Cincinnati, OH 45202-2434: 513-421-1420.

National Academy of Recording Arts and Sciences (NARAS), 303 North Glen Oaks Boulevard, Suite 140 Mezzanine, Burbank, CA 91502-1178: 213-849-1313.

National Academy of Songwriters, 6381 Hollywood Boulevard, Suite 780, Hollywood, CA 90028: 213-463-7178.

National Association for Music Therapy, 505 11th Street SE, Washington, DC 20003: 202-543-6864.

National Association of Band Instrument Manufacturers, c/o Jerry Hershman, 136 West 21st Street, New York, NY 10011: 212-924-9175.

National Association of Broadcast Employees and Technicians, AFL-CIO, 7101 Wisconsin Avenue, Suite 800, Bethesda, MD 20814: 301-657-8420.

National Association of Broadcasters, 1771 N Street, NW, Washington, DC 20036, 202-429-5300.

National Association of College Wind and Percussion Instructors, Dr. Richard Weerts, Executive Secretary, c/o Division of Fine Arts, Northeast Missouri State University, Kirksville, MO 63501: 816-785-4442.

National Association of Composers/USA, PO Box 49652, Barrington Station, Los Angeles, CA 90049: 213-541-8213.

National Association of Music Importers and Exporters, 136 West 21st Street, New York, NY 10011: 212-924-9175.

National Association of Music Merchants, 5140 Avenida Encinas, Carlsbad, CA 92008, 619-438-8001.

National Association of Professional Band Instrument Repair Technicians, PO Box 51, Normal, IL 61761: 309-452-4257.

National Association of Recording Merchandisers, 3 Eves Drive, Suite 307, Marlton, NJ 08053: 609-596-2221.

National Association of School Music Dealers, c/o Paul Heid, 308 E. College Avenue, Appleton, WI 54912: 414-734-0461.

National Association of Schools of Music, 11250 Roger Bacon Drive #21, Reston, VA 22090: 703-437-0700.

National Band Association, c/o L. Howard, Nicar, PO Box 121292, Nashville, TN 37212: 615-343-4775.

National Council of State Supervisors of Music, 1902 Association Drive, Reston, VA 22091-1597: 703-860-4000.

National Music Council, 40 West 34th Street, Suite 1010, New York, NY 10001: 212-563-3734.

National Music Publishers Association, 205 East 42nd Street, 18th Floor, New York, NY 10017: 212-370-5330.

National Orchestral Association, 475 Riverside Drive, Room 249, New York, NY 1011: 212-870-2009.

National Piano Foundation, c/o Don Dillon Associates, 4020 McEwen #105, Dallas, TX 75244-5019: 214-233-9107.

National School Orchestra Association, 345 Maxwell Drive, Pittsburgh, PA 15236: 412-882-6696.

National Symphony Orchestra Association, JFK Center for the Performing Arts, Washington, DC 20566: 202-416-8100.

Organization of American Kodály Educators, Music Department, Nicholls State University, Box 2017, Thibodaux, LA 70310: 504-446-8111 x255.

Piano Manufacturers Association International, c/o Don Dillon Associates, 4020 McEwen #105, Dallas, TX 75244-5019: 214-233-9107.

Piano Technicians Guild, 4510 Belleview, Suite 100, Kansas City, MO 64111: 816-753-7747.

Production Music Library Association, 40 East 49th Street, 9th Floor, New York, NY 10017: 212-832-1098.

Recording Industry Association of America, 1020 19th Street NW, Suite 200, Washington, DC 20036: 202-775-0101.

Retail Sheet Music Dealers Association, c/o Don Dillon Associates, 4020 McEwen #105, Dallas, TX 75244-5019: 214-233-9107.

Royal School of Church Music, Addington Palace, Croyden, Surrey, England CR9 5AD

Sacred Music Magazine, c/o Rev. Msgr. Richard J. Schuler, 548 Lafond Avenue, St. Paul, MN 55103: 612-293-1710.

Shepherd School of Music, Rice University, PO Box 1892, Houston, TX 77251-1892: 713-527-4854.

Simpson, Baldwin Piano and Organ Co., 422 Ward's Corner Road, Loveland, OH 45140: 513-576-4665.

Society of European Songwriters, Authors and Composers (SESAC), 55 Music Square East, Nashville, TN 37203: 615-320-0055.

The Songwriters Guild of America, 276 Fifth Avenue, Room 306, New York, NY 10001: 212-686-6820.

Suzuki Association of the Americas, PO Box 354, Muscatine, IA 52761-0354: 319-263-3071.

Tanglewood Music Center, Symphony Hall, Boston, MA 02115: 617-266-5241.

United States Army Band, Chief, Army Bands, Attn: ATZI-AB, Fort Benjamin Harrison, IN 46216-5070: 317-542-4723.

United States Coast Guard Band, U.S. Coast Guard Academy (pb), 15 Mohegan Avenue, New London, CT 06320-4195: 203-444-8466.

United States Marine Band ("The President's Own"), Attn: Operations Officer, Marine Barracks, 8th and I Streets, SE, Washington, DC 20390-5000: 202-433-5714.

United States Navy Bands, Head, Music Branch (NMPC-654), Naval Military Personnel Command, Washington, DC 20370-5654: 202-746-7000.

Volunteer Lawyers for the Arts, 1285 Avenue of the Americas, Third Floor, New York, NY 10019: 212-977-9270.

Women Band Directors National Association, 344 Overlook Drive, West Lafayette, IN 47906: 317-463-1738.

1011-12-5M-8/90